Frederick Douglass (Photo courtesy of Atlanta University Center Archives.)

# The Dream Deferred

# A Survey of Black America

# 1840 - 1896

## Second Edition

Berman E. Johnson

**KENDALL/HUNT PUBLISHING COMPANY**
4050 Westmark Drive        Dubuque, Iowa 52002

For

David

George

and

Rosemary

# Contents

# Foreword

During the eight years that Berman Johnson and I served as administrators for DeKalb College and DeKalb Technical Institute, questions related to race relations often surfaced in our decisions affecting students and the community. The most prominent was: During the development of America's personality and character, was there ever an opportunity to bring the races together to form the perfect union aspired to in the United States Constitution? As former professors in United States history, we generally agreed that the 1840-1896 period presented a volatile environment and ideal conditions that were not fully utilized for social progress. In fact, we concluded that if the nation in that period had not frittered away excellent opportunities to live out its creed of liberty, justice, and equality, race relations in America would be decidedly improved today.

We postulated that the realization of this creed was the dream of founding fathers like George Washington and Thomas Jefferson just as it was a half century later for abolitionists like Frederick Douglass, William Lloyd Garrison, and Harriet Tubman. Although the 1840-1896 period saw the eradication of slavery, it also saw the dream deferred for later generations. Moreover, the tabling of human rights for all Americans reduced blacks to a nadir of existence in that period, and racial polarization left a legacy of social problems that continue one hundred years later.

Dr. Johnson's major concern is that in its aversion to serious, grass root studies in American history the present generation may fail to heed the lessons and admonitions of the 1840-1896 period, and consequently future generations may be doomed to repeat its failures. He thus surveys the period in honest attempts to explode the myths which have perpetuated racial disunity, and he and chides historians who have contributed to basic misconceptions about African Americans.

This short survey is recommended supplementary reading for courses related to American history. In the domain of American race relations, it shows why we are where we are, and it meaningfully focuses on pitfalls that should be avoided to gainfully shape the future.

Eugene P. Walker

Commissioner, Georgia Department
of Children and Youth Services

# Acknowledgments

The author wishes to express his thanks to the following persons:

Dr. George Faust, for requiring me to write a major research paper which stimulated my interest in the 1840-1896 period.

Dr. John Cary, for steering my graduate research on blacks during the Civil War.

Professor Curtis Wilson and Dr. Melvin Drimmer, for sagaciously taught courses on black America which bolstered my graduate studies in United States history.

Jacqueline D. Scruggs, for editorial comments which were invaluable for revisions of the manuscript.

Thomas R. Henderson, Kenneth A. Smoke, Leanne M. White, Robert Green, and Jumiah A. Johnston for their technical assistance in the preparation of this book.

*What happens to a dream deferred?*
*Does it dry up*
*like a raisin in the sun?*
                    *Langston Hughes-1951*

# Introduction

## I

When the United States was established in 1787, the new nation embarked upon a bold venture that set new precedents for social development. Never before had a government vested sovereign power to the people, promoted a succession without hereditary leadership or privileges, and developed a written Constitution with a Bill of Rights to protect civil liberties. This federal system was designed to prevent anyone or any group from exercising excessive power, and it was built upon 150 years of colonial experience and vassalage to Great Britain. Civil liberties subsequently became the cornerstone of the nation and an exemplar for world-wide emulation. Also, civil liberties became most important to American citizens. They were designed to address the perceived shortfalls in colonialism, and they began to be referred to by the founding fathers as the American Dream.

The American Dream has grown to epitomize the democratic ideals and aspirations on which the United States was founded, and it is usually meant to express the American way of life at its best. Its definition varies because everyone has different dreams; however, as a force behind government philosophy the American Dream is primarily interpreted as a combination of freedom and opportunity with increasing overtones of civil liberties and social justice. Concurrently, it refers to American opportunities and goals of having a better lifestyle than the previous generation, property ownership, and to the ability to comfortably rear and educate one's children. Missed opportunities for realizing the American Dream therefore require serious reflections upon those factors which contribute to the deferred Dream.

Black people in America had no voice in the process of establishing the nation and had little hope in participating in the American Dream embodied in the Bill of Rights. Neither did women or other ethnic minorities, and because of property restrictions and a lack of education, only one-fourth of the

American white male population was represented in the process. The 55 men who drafted the United States Constitution made it crystal clear that they meant to establish an oligarchical rule where the majority of the population would have no voice. They were men of property and position whose main concern was order and stability. Their contention was that the masses should be content with their conditions and be grateful that an enlightened electorate was looking out for their welfare and best interests. This inconsistency with the spirit of the United States Constitution was not greatly debated in the 1780s; the most pressing issue was the division of power between the federal and the state governments.

In 1790 the United States had a population of 3,929,214 of which 758,338 (19.3 percent) were black. There were 59,000 persons who were recognized as free blacks. Blacks had arrived before the 1620s and had served primarily as laborers for a white population too small to sustain an economy on their own; however, blacks in the South performed in every skilled trade known in colonial America. Blacks had fought bravely in the American Revolutionary War (1776-1883) which won the right to establish the nation, and they had painfully endured their consignment to slavery while other laborers (white indentured servants) were provided avenues to obtain freedom and participation as American citizens. Moreover, the founding fathers including James Madison, who was the greatest contributor to the United States Constitution and the most creative political thinker of his generation, helped to set the tenor of the new Republic by writing eloquent justifications for the notion of black inferiority and the legal treatment of slaves as property.

The First Industrial Revolution in the early 1800s unleashed forces which encouraged the northern states to abolish slavery; however, those same forces promoted the expansion of slavery in the southern states to the extent that the slave population more than quadrupled in the first 30 years of the new Republic. The free black population also grew in the early 1800s but their lot was reduced to a miserable existence where they lived on the fringes of society, "a third element in a system designed for two." Even liberal white Americans who sought a solution to "the Negro problem" never advanced the sharing of civil liberties with free blacks as a suitable alternative. Instead, they often called for the complete removal of all free blacks from the United States and engineered schemes to relocate them (on a voluntary basis) to the west coast of Africa. Some free blacks chose to emigrate but the overwhelming majority chose to stay in the United States.

At no time did free blacks in the North offer any concerted militant resistance to the structure which denied them civil liberties. They recognized that the abolition of slavery would have to take place first, and prominent free blacks such as Benjamin Banneker, Prince Hall, Richard Allen, and Absolum Jones wrote strong letters of appeal to the authorities. But in the South free blacks did not completely acquiesce to the denial of civil liberties, and their presence contributed to slave revolts and conspiracies which generated a wave of fear and apprehension in southern society. Their resistance spoke to the denial of civil liberties in a nation where white Americans boasted freedom, liberty, and equality, and at the same time openly praised the revolutions and demonstrations for civil liberties then emerging in Europe and Latin America.

Unlike Brazil where the struggle for civil liberties resulted in standing slave armies engaged in open rebellion and guerilla warfare against authorities, slave resistance in the United States was more contained. American slave populations were more heterogeneous as slave owners were careful not to install whole tribes of slaves in a given area. Confusion among the slaves was encouraged. Slaves often spoke several African dialects on a large plantation and they were not allowed to assemble in large groups. Also, the education of slaves was prohibited. These conditions greatly contributed to keeping slave revolts from spreading to large areas.

Despite these measures, resistance to slavery, revolts, and conspiracies were a common occurrence during the entire history of slavery in the United States. The three conspiracies which have been given the most attention were those in 1800, 1822, and 1831 primarily because of their potential for spreading across the South. In 1800 Gabriel Prosser, a free black preacher in Henrico County, Virginia just outside of Richmond, planned for months to take over the city. Virginia had the largest black population in the nation and more than three times as many blacks as South Carolina which had the second largest black population. Virginia's free black population in 1800 outnumbered the slaves by a three to one ratio because of rewards and manumissions generated from the Revolutionary War. Prosser and a host of free blacks gathered clubs, swords, and other weapons, and then assembled with over 1,000 slaves to march on Richmond on August 30, 1800. But a violent storm took place and routed the insurgents; however, two turncoat slaves had already alerted the authorities and the state militia. After they were apprehended, the calm and reserve shown by the slave leaders in the trials that followed the uprising served to unnerve whites. Prosser refused to talk to anyone and indicated a readiness to suffer the consequences of his actions. He and 35 slave leaders were executed and many others were arrested and implicated in the plot, including two white men.

In 1820 Denmark Vesey, a free black Methodist preacher in an integrated church in Charleston, South Carolina, devised a scheme for the slaves nearby to seize Charleston, burn it, and sail away to freedom. He had immigrated from St. Thomas in the Virgin Islands, worked as a carpenter, and enjoyed a relatively comfortable living. But his concern for blacks in slavery and the ideas of freedom from the new black Republic of Haiti led him to conspire with a white supporter, and over a period of several years he and his carefully chosen assistants secured guns, pike heads, bayonets, and daggers in preparation for the revolt. He set a Sunday in July 1822 for the day of revolt with a force of 9,000 men; however, a turncoat slave alerted the authorities in time to foil the plot. Vesey and 139 blacks were arrested, 47 were condemned, and four white men were fined or imprisoned for encouraging the conspiracy.

Vesey's trial was significant to southern white Christians because it served to define their stand on slavery. Previously, white Methodists in the South had frowned on slavery, but Vesey's plot was to kill all whites in Charleston regardless of their religious persuasions. Southern white clergy was then forced by public opinion to endorse slavery and began to seek rationales to contain its doctrine of black inferiority in Christian teachings. Subsequently, they moved into the pro-slavery camp and became slavery's firmest supporters.

The Prosser and Vesey conspiracies ran concurrent with a new trend where civil liberties were becoming more of an issue to white Americans who also began to question slavery. Although these conspiracies accelerated fear in the South, they fell short of shedding the blood of white Americans. Such was not the case in the 1831 Nat Turner insurrection when over 60 whites were killed. This insurrection was precipitated by the incendiary publications of David Walker and William Lloyd Garrison who challenged the United States Constitution and began the first call for black freedom.

David Walker was a free black used clothes salesman in Boston who had lived in North Carolina. In 1829 he wrote an essay entitled: "Walker's Appeal in Four Articles Together with a Preamble to the Colored Citizens of the World But in Particular and very Expressly to those of the United States of America." It was the most penetrating denouncement on slavery ever printed in the nation, and he called for all blacks to revolt and overthrow the system of slavery. He sent his essay to all the major periodicals and editors in the South; Savannah, Georgia alone received 50 copies. Walker's *Appeal* quoted the 1776 United States Declaration of Independence in justifying forceful black resistance against white oppression. The entire nation was shocked by the audacity of a black man who dared to call for militant action against whites. Southerners wrote letters of complaint to Massachusetts demanding his arrest and imprisonment, and their paranoid reaction gave Walker's *Appeal* more notoriety and attention than it would ordinarily have received.

William Lloyd Garrison's writings were even more intimidating to whites North and South. In January 1831 he began publication of the *Liberator* in Boston. Garrison was the first white man to break the "conspiracy of silence" which had protected the system of slavery. He was militant and uncompromising, and he invoked the Declaration of Independence to claim that blacks as well as whites were entitled to life, liberty, and the pursuit of happiness. He mailed his *Liberator* to more than 100 periodicals; however, it was not widely read in the North except among free blacks. But in the South the *Liberator* caused near mass hysteria. Southern legislators and governors demanded his immediate arrest and imprisonment, a bounty was set upon his head, and southern editors assailed him in the press relentlessly. Garrison subsequently became the most eloquent spokesman for non-violent militant abolition and he served as the President of the American Anti-Slavery Society for 25 years.

Nat Turner's insurrection occurred in Southampton County, Virginia where he was born a slave. As a child prodigy who taught himself to read, he was very religious, precocious, observant, and convinced that he was a Messiah sent by God to eliminate slavery. His divine claim led him to be accepted as a preacher. When he became an adult he escaped from slavery, but within 30 days he voluntarily returned to fulfill a mission that he could not yet identify. Thereafter, he began to have visions which called upon him to conduct an armed insurrection against slavery. Turner was not a violent person but after claiming to see a sign from God on August 21, 1831, he and his followers proceeded to kill his master and his master's family and within 24 hours more than 60 whites were killed. The insurrection rapidly spread and state and federal troops were called to overwhelm the insurgents, resulting in more than 100 slaves killed, as well as 13 slaves and three free blacks hanged immediately. Two months later Turner was captured and executed.

The Nat Turner insurrection generated stark terror in the South because it could not be determined if it was a single sporadic event or part of a well-planned general uprising. Many southerners blamed Walker's *Appeal* and the *Liberator* precipitating several states to call special sessions for their legislatures to consider the emergency. After 1832 southern legislatures enacted provisions for the legal protection of slavery and laws were passed prohibiting the circulation of anti-slavery literature. Maryland made it a high offense to write or circulate publications showing a tendency to create discontent among blacks, and it became a felony for free blacks to receive abolition newspapers through any post office. South Carolina made it a crime to subscribe to any literature "calculated to disaffect" the slaves, and Arkansas prescribed terms in the penitentiary for those who challenged the right of property for slave owners. Slave Codes were tightened as the South installed a "cotton curtain" barring any internal or external debate on slavery.

This massive assault on civil liberties was not confined to black people; it also included Native Americans in the South whose property rights were summarily ignored. In 1838 the United States government joined this debacle by assisting in the forcible removal of the entire Cherokee Nation where 4,000 died in the "Trail of Tears," one of the shameful episodes in American history.

The South was the dominant force in the nation in the early decades of the 1800s, and in that role it would serve as a poor caretaker of civil liberties. The South saw a desperate need to defend slavery even at the cost of civil liberties for its white citizens; consequently, the most effective defense was the preaching and rationalization of black inferiority. Thus the fortunes of all blacks North and South, slave and free, were aligned and intensified to abolish slavery. The preaching and rationalization of black inferiority required a repetitious assault upon the tenets embodied in the United States Constitution and it also required a twisted logic that was at odds with itself. As writer Louis Lomax would say more than 100 years later, "If the law-abiding rather than the lawbreakers must cease and desist, then the American promise is but a cruel joke on humanity and the American dream dissolves to the most God-awful nightmare."

By 1840 the United States had become a loose confederation of 26 states with a population of just over 17 million, little central authority, and very few notable sectional differences. However, in the 1840s and 1850s sectional differences became more important while efforts towards national unity and economic competition began to identify two distinct homogeneous cultures: the North and the South. Implicit in the union, however, was the dream that all men were endowed with the rights of life, liberty, and the pursuit of happiness.

The greatest distinction between the two sections was their labor systems. The industrial North was committed to a free-labor economy while the agricultural South institutionalized slavery as its primary source of labor. The two systems might have co-existed peaceably had they not been affected by the tensions and conflicts brought to the surface by western expansion and the abolition movement. The nation thus entered the second half of the nineteenth century with a challenge to realize the American Dream and to bring its 2,873,648 black population -- as well as the white South -- into the mainstream of a common culture.

The period of 1840-1896 reflects abortive attempts to make the American Dream a reality. The period contains the antebellum years, Civil War and Reconstruction, and the years of southern redemption. This survey reviews the major events during this time which assured that the Dream would be deferred. It also demonstrates how those events served to crystallize racial stereotypes which impede social progress in twentieth-century America.

The survey is taken from a compendium of books many of which were published by revisionist historians who conscientiously brought forth more plausible interpretations of American history in the 1960s. It also contains information from sources contemporary with the 1840-1896 period. These facts and perceptions are synthesized with an updated assessment of conditions inherited from that period. Those conditions since the 1960s include the systematic exclusion of the study of African American history and the influx of black awareness related to race pride.

Studies in African American history and black awareness were virtually nonexistent during the period of 1840-1896. From the 1840s when the abolition movement rolled into high gear to the Plessy V. Ferguson Decision of 1896 when black hopes for assimilation began to fade, most blacks aspired to become a part of the American "melting pot," and they provided little agitation commensurate with race pride. Even the valiant efforts made by blacks in the Civil War were concerted attempts to be recognized and accepted as full-fledged American citizens. But the tragedy of the Reconstruction Era, southern redemption, and the Atlanta Compromise served to legally consign blacks to a position of servitude. By 1896 the Plessy V. Ferguson Decision wrote second-class citizenship into federal law, and it appeared that the large number of blacks who had fought and died for full citizenship did so in vain. Also, by 1896 African American history became even more distorted, and black awareness had to wait until the 1960s to become a socially acceptable concept.

It appears that the proliferation of African American history has not been as fruitful as revisionist historians of the 1960s had hoped for. However, studies in African American history have served to eradicate many long-standing racial stereotypes. African American history is now celebrated for an entire month and is recognized in many educational systems throughout the nation. Despite this celebration and recognition, however, each year many high school and college students graduate without gaining any knowledge about black America.

The celebration of African American history should result in its study, especially among black people. If the celebration does not move black people to study their roots, it has limited meaning and potential. It is almost ludicrous that black people would celebrate an honored past that they know little or nothing about. Indeed, such celebration unaccompanied by efforts in study and knowledge-seeking smacks of racial chauvinism. It borders on an ethnic ego trip which can serve little constructive purpose in a multicultural, multiracial environment.

*The Dream Deferred* concentrates on 1840 through 1896 because that time was a critical, pivotal period in United States history where black people were taught a fundamental sociodynamic lesson: Full citizenship is never freely given to an oppressed people; it must be coveted and pursued with deliberate, persistent agitation. Few blacks in that period were of a mind set to learn that lesson, and its appeal did not reach the masses until after the 1960s when the interpretations of revisionist historians began to be more widely accepted. The study of black America must increase if that lesson is to be passed to future generations, and if the battle for human rights and equal treatment is to continue. The Dream will remain deferred until all Americans -- regardless of their skin color -- can walk with dignity and purpose in the land.

The term "black America" is used to describe collectively the people of African ancestry who have lived in America since its founding. They have invariably been referred to in the literature as blacks, negroes, colored, and most recently African Americans. In the text, I have taken the posture that since these people were not American citizens until 1868, they were simply blacks, slave and free, who lived in America. Consistent with that posture which also alludes to their precarious circumstances, I generally refer to the people of black America as "blacks" prior to 1868 and as "African Americans" thereafter.

Many historians contend that it is difficult to understand America unless you have studied its Civil War. I posit that it is virtually impossible to understand America unless you have studied American slavery, Civil War and Reconstruction, and southern redemption. Therein lies the central purpose and intent of this survey, and its brief number of pages is meant to encourage readers who are less inspired by traditional writings in history.

Berman E. Johnson

# CHAPTER I

## Antebellum Free Blacks

*This is called "the land of the free and the home of the brave "...*
*... and some have been foolish enough to call it the "Cradle of Liberty."*
*If it is the "Cradle of Liberty," they have rocked the child to death.*
William Wells Brown-1847

Black America in 1840 had many vestiges of an uprooted people who were bonded and subjugated by an oppressive force. This was apparent not only for the vast majority of blacks who were slaves, it also held true for so-called "free negroes" who lived under the most precarious conditions.

The plight of black America in 1840 could be described as follows: (1) the slave system was secure, (2) frustrated abolitionists quarreled among themselves about tactics and methodology, (3) civil rights for free blacks were steadily being eroded, (4) a strong movement prevailed to remove the entire free black population out of the United States, and (5) most liberal whites were convinced that the two races could never live together in peace. Indeed, in the second decade prior to the Civil War there were virtually no indications that black America could ever become a part of the mainstream of American culture and society.

There were 386,293 blacks in the United States who were not designated as being slaves in 1840. These free blacks represented 13 percent of the black population and 2 percent of the nation's total population. Half of the free blacks lived in the South and they included many well- to-do persons who tended to develop a stable and patrifocal pattern of family life comparable to that of whites. The population of free blacks was increased by offspring from interracial unions, offspring from free black parents, and legalized manumission. During the early years of the United States, the growth of the free black population was rapid amounting to about three times the growth of the slave population. But after 1810 the trend reversed as slavery began to make its full impact on the nation to become institutionalized by 1830.

The free black population was distributed in seven characteristic areas: (1) the Tidewater Region of Virginia and Maryland; (2) the Piedmont Region of North Carolina and Virginia; (3) the seaboard cities of Charleston, South Carolina, Mobile, Alabama, and New Orleans, Louisiana; (4) the northern cities including Boston, New York, Chicago, Cincinnati, Philadelphia, Baltimore, and Washington, D.C.; (5) the Northwest Territory; (6) isolated communities of blacks mixed with Native Americans; and (7) the Seminole Territory of Florida (Frazier, 1932).

## Southern Free Blacks

State laws varied concerning free blacks in the South. A Mississippi law passed in 1822 limited manumission to cases validated by a special act of the legislature in which the slave had performed some meritorious act for the owner or the state. But in Maryland manumission was more easily accepted. Consequently, Maryland had the largest free black population in the nation (52,938 in 1830 and 83,942 in 1860). Southern free blacks shied away from rural areas and mainly resided in cities which provided a different life from the plantation system.

The most striking characteristic of free black communities was the prominence of the mulatto element. In 1850, 37 percent of the free black population were classed as mulattoes while only eight percent of the slave population was of mixed blood. This increase was largely caused by the union of slave

2

women and white men who manumitted their mulatto offspring. In Florida the Seminoles were so mixed with blacks that the conflict between the United States Government and the Seminoles was partly an attempt by Native American fathers to prevent their children born of black mothers from being enslaved by their white neighbors (Frazier, 1932).

Urban area free blacks were able to secure some formal education. The urban environment also offered free blacks an opportunity to enter a variety of occupations which gave them economic security and independence in some cases. During the antebellum period, Virginia's free blacks were the most prosperous because of manufacturing prevalent in the state. Throughout the South free blacks in the antebellum period could make contracts and own property. They did not have to compete with white immigrants who generally avoided slave labor areas, and in southern cities most of the work in the mechanical trades was engaged by free blacks (Quarles, 1964).

Wealthy free blacks were rare but there were some, notably in New Orleans where free blacks were more advanced than in any other city. Some free blacks owned slaves, but mostly for paternal and not for commercial reasons. The newly manumitted free black was usually required to leave the state, but with a black master relatives could be retained in a benevolent and temporary ownership.

Free blacks in New Orleans left a legacy of achievement in military affairs, science, and literature. Even before the Louisiana Purchase of 1803 two black regiments were in existence in New Orleans. They fought with Andrew Jackson and received commendations for their courage and perseverance. In 1846 Norbert Rilleux, a New Orleans free black, produced a vacuum cup that revolutionized sugar refining methods, an act for which he is still acclaimed by the sugar corporations of the world. Victor Sejour, another free black of New Orleans, was a talented poet and playwright who achieved great fame in France. His achievements provided considerable prestige for free blacks in the South. Some social distinctions were set up by these black bourgeoisie which were similar to those established all over the nation and they included skin color, occupation, schooling, and free ancestry.

Blacks whose skin color closely approximated that of whites were generally held in highest esteem. However, these distinctions within the black society were private and not matters of public policy. Free blacks were politically powerless and could not transpose any of these prejudgments and race concepts into law. But the concept of white as representing all that was good, clean, noble, and true, and the concept of black as representing all that was evil, dirty, and inferior was indelibly pronounced in the free black society.

Restrictions for free southern blacks varied from state to state. In addition, they vacillated from one extreme to another based upon the race relations of the times. Nowhere in the South could blacks come and go as they pleased because all southern states had laws forbidding immigration. Typical of states enacting laws to this effect was Maryland's Act passed in 1839. A free black entering Maryland without permission was fined $20 for the first offense and up to $500 for the second offense. If he could not pay these fines, he could be sold as a slave to the highest bidder (Quarles, 1964).

Free blacks were not permitted to possess firearms unless by special permit. In Kentucky they could not buy liquor except through a reputable white person, and in Georgia and Florida a free black had to have a white guardian to whom he was required to report periodically. Like slaves, free blacks were denied the right of assembly except in church and they were forced to observe a curfew in every southern state. Free blacks had to always carry a certificate of freedom which had to be renewed periodically. Blacks who lost these papers were customarily treated as runaway slaves and resold to slave trading firms.

After the Nat Turner slave revolt of 1831 in Southampton County, Virginia, the slave states were beset with rumors of uprisings. Sometimes this apprehension reached the proportion of mass hysteria which could only be relieved by seizing, convicting, and condemning a number of innocent free blacks. The southern states tightened their restrictions on free blacks whom many felt were as dangerous as the revolt-minded slaves. Free blacks could be reduced to slavery if they failed to pay their debts, taxes, fines, or court fees. They could not hold public office and could not vote in most southern states. Free blacks began to vote in Tennessee in 1834 and in North Carolina in 1835. In most states they could not testify against a white man in a civil court case.

## Northern Free Blacks

Free blacks in the northern states of Ohio, Illinois, and Indiana were little better off than those in the South. Ohio passed a law in 1807 to regulate black and mulatto persons that was similar to the most stringent laws of southern states. The doctrine of white supremacy was held almost as tenaciously in the North as it was in the South. Free blacks were regarded as a threat to the general welfare and were treated as a social liability; however, blacks in the North could protest and had greater opportunity for self-expression through their participation in churches, newspapers, and conventions.

Free blacks also participated in reform movements. The Negro Convention Movement took place during the three decades prior to the Civil War and the most notable black leaders of the time participated in it. The Convention Movement was a series of meetings designed to improve the conditions of free blacks in the United States, to provide them a sense of direction, to establish priorities, and to coordinate their efforts. They were not permanent associations and they were never attended by more than 150 delegates at one meeting. In the 1840s the meetings stressed the need for full political equality and even advocated slave uprisings. In the mid-1850s they stressed complete separatism and a massive black emigration from America. But the Convention Movement suffered from divided leadership, conflicting programs, and confusion over means and ends. Although it never realized its goals of political, social, and economic equality, the Convention Movement produced a variety of able black leaders and set three major enduring strands of reform and protest thought: individual assimilation, communal integrative action, and separation (W.H. Pease and J.H. Pease, 1971).

Because their numbers were small in the North, free blacks did not arouse the degree of uneasiness and dread that they did in the South. Thus, it is significant that in 1840 the black population was smallest in the four states where blacks had some equal status --Massachusetts, Maine, New Hampshire, and

William Lloyd Garrison, prominent white northern abolitionist, spoke so vehemently in his newspaper against slavery that the Georgia legislature offered $4,000 for his arrest. (Photo courtesy of Atlanta University Center Archives.)

Vermont. However, except in Massachusetts, free blacks in these states were debarred from jury service.

Northern free blacks faced fierce competition from white immigrants in making a living, and were generally confined to jobs as common laborers or as domestic servants. Many former slaves were already skilled artisans when they arrived in the United States; thus they transferred their skills into viable trades and occupations that were prevalent in the South. However, they found that as free men in the North they could not put their training to use. Trade unions refused to accept black applicants and employers feared reprisals from white workers if they hired a skilled black man. After 1840 when white immigrants arrived in the United States in larger numbers, even unskilled jobs such as porter, waiter, cook, and maid were difficult for blacks to obtain. In California free blacks faced added competition from Chinese immigrants who would work for very low wages.

Despite these hindrances some northern blacks prospered as caterers, restaurant owners, barbers, and farmers. In the West they became conspicuous in the fur trade conducted from St. Louis. Also, free blacks were employed as cooks, voyagers, hunters, guides, interpreters, and traders. A prime example was James Beckwourth who in 1850 discovered the lowest point across the Northern Sierra-Nevada mountains (Beckwourth Pass). Another example was Jean Baptiste Point du Sable, the first permanent settler on the present site of Chicago.

A small minority of free blacks favored colonization to Liberia because they could not fully participate as citizens in the United States. But the overwhelming majority insisted on staying in America to fight for emancipation. Such was the sentiment of Robert Purvis who helped found *The Liberator* with William Lloyd Garrison, the most notable white abolitionist of the period. Purvis was a black organizer of several anti-slavery societies. He was heir to his wealthy white father's fortune, and he appeared white but identified with blacks. He felt that American backing of the Liberian colony was a way to remove free blacks and thus make slavery more secure. Many blacks whose skin color approximated that of

Harriet Beecher Stowe wrote *Uncle Tom's Cabin* and caused such a furor against slavery that President Abraham Lincoln reportedly described her as the "little woman who brought on the Civil War." (Photo courtesy of William L. Katz Collection.)

William Wells Brown, an escaped slave who became an active conductor of the Underground Railroad and America's first black novelist and playwright. (Photo courtesy of William L. Katz Collection.)

whites migrated to another state to pass for white, thus blending into the vast melting pot to escape northern racism.

Colonization to Africa and the Caribbean Islands was the focus of an important but futile effort to end slavery. The American Colonization Society was organized in 1817 by a group of prominent white Virginians, and it spread nationwide to form local and state chapters in the North. The Society proposed a gradual freeing of slaves with masters receiving monetary compensation from private donors, state legislatures, and the United States Congress. And to some extent they were successful. Congress and the state legislatures of Virginia and Maryland aided the Society which arranged for the shipment of several groups of blacks out of the country. By 1830 the Society had established the nation of Liberia primarily for the purpose of having a designated place to relocate free blacks. Equally important, the Society unwittingly contributed to the college education of a number of free blacks.

In the antebellum period, only a handful of colleges would accept blacks as students; however, the Society influenced the enrollment of selected free blacks who had a potential for leadership and who promised to emigrate to Africa in return for their college education. The Society was convinced that establishing a group of well-educated aspiring black leaders would stimulate colonization. Other blacks would then be encouraged to emigrate with these newfound black leaders to areas such as Africa and the Caribbean Islands where they purportedly had more opportunities to function as free men. By 1865 approximately 350 blacks received college training through these efforts and several free blacks in antebellum America earned baccalaureate degrees from notable institutions such as Princeton University, Dartmouth College, and especially Oberlin College (Irvine, 1996). They were duly informed, however, that they were not being educated for leadership roles in America, but for leadership roles in other undeveloped parts of the world.

The Society's mission was to solve the "race problem" by removing the black population from the United States. It was unsuccessful because the task was insurmountable, most white planters were not eager to allow their slaves to abandon their plantations (but they were in favor of sending all free blacks back to Africa), and most free blacks bitterly resisted coloniza-

9

tion. A number of talented free blacks promised that they would emigrate to Africa but after securing a college education sponsored by the Society they reneged on their pledge to leave the United States to join the abolition movement. Thus, the abortive attempt made by the Society helped to form a cadre of black intelligentsia which bolstered the ranks of black abolitionists who labored to end slavery through vastly different means.

Nearly all schools in the North refused to accept free blacks as students. The few segregated schools that accepted them were funded grudgingly and held in some black church edifice with less than adequate teachers and equipment. Jim Crow laws which legally segregated the races was rampant as free blacks were debarred from nearly all public accommodations. Denied the opportunity of securing an education, blacks were upbraided in private and in public for their ignorance. Even the white churches treated free blacks as though they were incorrigible. The northern white churches were applauded as a refuge for the unfortunate and the afflicted. But when it came to rights for free blacks, the churches were the last institutions in the country to take a position on the subject. Even then it was a moderate position that reflected the racism of antebellum white Christians in the North.

Black participation in the fine arts was severely limited in the antebellum period. An undisclosed number of blacks left the United States during slavery in order to participate in the arts. In drama Ira Frederick Aldridge fled America for Europe where he gained fame in such leading roles as Shakespeare's Othello, King Lear, and many others. His place of honor is acknowledged today at The Shakespeare Memorial Theater and many crowned heads of Europe paid tribute to his performances.

Black talent during slavery was also frustrated and misplaced in other areas. James Madison Bell was a black abolitionist poet who migrated in 1854 to California where he helped support John Brown's anti-slavery activities. His potential literary talent remained undeveloped because of his preoccupation for abolition, and his poetry which evoked considerable interest was not published as a collection until 1901. Robert Duncanson was one of the ablest painters in his time; however, after gaining some fame in Cincinnati he found it necessary to migrate to Europe to obtain full recognition as an artist.

Elizabeth Taylor Greenfield, known as "the Black Swan of the concert stage," was born in Natchez, Mississippi. She was taken to Philadelphia, Pennsylvania as a child by a Quaker lady who later discovered that she had a gifted voice. Her voice had flexibility as well as unusual range and her control was phenomenal for an untrained vocalist. Her tours in the northern states and in Europe attracted many prominent admirers including Great Britain's Queen Victoria, and she had a close relationship with novelist Harriet Beecher Stowe.

Up until 1865 there was a steady flow of black literature destined in advance to be still-born. Moreover, it was created in defiance of the laws making literacy for slaves a crime. It consisted of autobiographies and narratives written and told by fugitive slaves. The apex of this literature is reflected in narratives by Frederick Douglass, William Wells Brown, and Samuel Ringgold Ward who were also black leaders in the anti-slavery movement.

These authors also contributed heavily to *The Freedom's Journal*, the first black newspaper in the United States which was published in New York City. *The Freedom's Journal* was designed to be a channel of communication between blacks and whites; however, it soon became the voice of growing dissatisfaction and was the forerunner of the anti-slavery struggle and the black abolitionist movement. Alain Locke, a notable black writer, has observed:

"If slavery molded the emotional and folk life of the Negro, it was the anti-slavery struggle that developed his intellect and spurred him to disciplined, articulate expression. Up to the Civil War, the growing anti-slavery movement was the midwife of Negro political and literary talent" (Chapman, 1968, p. 24).

## Black Abolitionists

Free blacks joined white abolitionists in an all out attack against slavery. Progress was slow and it seemed at times that the cause was lost. When the United States Supreme Court Dred Scott Decision of 1857 affirmed that no black person could legally claim to be a citizen of the United States,

11

SOJOURNER TRUTH.

From a Photograph, taken a short time before her death.

Sojourner Truth, notable Ohio abolitionist who traveled in the North giving lectures against slavery with a strange religious mysticism. (Photo courtest of Atlanta University Center Archives.)

free blacks North and South searched in vain for an alternative. Some chose colonization to Liberia, but most elected to follow the lead of Frederick Douglass whose militancy for freedom was tempered by a policy of non-violence. Free blacks devoted much of their energy toward changing public opinion against slavery, but some aided John Brown's attempts to bring about abolition by force of arms.

The abolition movement contained many free blacks in the North. The most prominent was Frederick Douglass, a former Maryland slave who escaped in 1838. For the next fifty years Douglass was the most prominent spokesmen for black people. From his newspaper *The North Star* published in Rochester, New York, he assailed slavery relentlessly. He advised President Abraham Lincoln on the possible role of blacks in the Civil War, and later held several important federal posts. A magnificent speaker, Douglass earned the respect of abolitionists at home and abroad with vivid accounts of his life as a slave in Maryland. Douglass stirred the hearts of all who listened and held a message of hope for those in bondage. In a lecture on slavery in Rochester on December 8, 1850 he proclaimed:

"While slavery exists, and the union of these states endures, every American citizen must bear the chagrin of hearing his country branded before the world as a Nation of liars and hypocrites; and behold his cherished National flag pointed at with the utmost scorn and derision" (Douglass, 1855, p. 438).

Douglass was also the most articulate black speaker of the nineteenth-century. His eloquence and his philosophical stance on social issues were so profound that many whites refused to believe that he was an unlettered former slave.

The abolition movement had many unsung black heroes such as William Cooper Nell who, when the Garrison camp split in 1840, banded free blacks together behind Garrison to further the fight for freedom. For many years Nell toiled inconspicuously behind the scenes and under the shadows of Douglass and Garrison. His efforts to mold public opinion against racism were profound, and his writings have been designated as:

". . . a clearer reflection of what was being done towards the development of the colored people as a social unit than were the better

13

known works of Douglass . . . " (Journal of Negro History, 1970, p. 196).

Black women were also prominent in the abolition movement. Mrs. Alexander Smith, a wealthy loan shark of San Francisco also known as Mammy Plessants, gave John Brown $30,000 to help finance the 1859 raid in Harpers Ferry, Virginia. Sojourner Truth, at a time when female orators were rare, was one of the most notable anti-slavery speakers of the North. Black women were strong supporters of the Underground Railroad, a society of black and white people who risked their lives and fortunes by establishing way stations for harboring runaway slaves.

The black abolitionists quarreled frequently among themselves about how best to further their cause. Douglass and Nell at times disagreed bitterly but both believed in a non-violent means to obtain emancipation. In this camp also was James W. C. Pennington, a fugitive slave who fled to New York and later received his Doctor of Divinity degree in Germany in the 1840s. Pennington spoke against slavery in front of aristocratic European audiences, and in the United States he and William Still fought discrimination in every affront to human dignity. Still was the Secretary of the Pennsylvania Society for the Abolition of Slavery and was active in the Underground Railroad.

William Whipper, another black Pennsylvanian, was the forerunner of non-violent resistance in America. One of the founders of the American Moral Reform Society, he was the editor of its official publication, *The National Reformer.* In 1837 he published his famous article, "An Address on Non-Resistance to Offensive Aggression" in which he stated that:

"the practice of non-resistance to physical aggression is not only consistent with reason, but the surest method of obtaining a speedy triumph of the principles of universal peace" (Biographical Sketches, 1970).

Whipper's theory on non-resistance was written 12 years before Henry David Thoreau's famous essay, "Civil Disobedience." Whipper was thus the forerunner of Thoreau, Mohandas K. Ghandi, and Martin Luther King, Jr., all of whom are highly acclaimed for their non-violent resistance.

The non-violent black abolitionists and many other free blacks worked with the anti-slavery societies exemplified by William Lloyd Garrison. Since white abolitionists enjoyed the fruits of citizenship, it was expedient for blacks to align their efforts with them. But it was the black abolitionist whose position was the most precarious in the so-called haven of freedom in the North. According to Williams:

> "Studied insolence jostled colored men and women from the streets of the larger (northern) cities; mobocratic violence broke up assemblages and churches of colored people; and malice sought them in the quiet of their homes -- outraged and slew them in cold blood" (1883, p. 170).

The militant black abolitionists were exemplified by Lewis Sheridan Leary who accompanied John Brown at Harpers Ferry, and James Forten, a wealthy veteran of the American Revolutionary War who used his fortune to fight for black civil rights. John Jones, a prominent Chicagoan and one of the wealthiest blacks in America, worked with John Brown and Douglass, and he was also active in the Underground Railroad. Militant blacks also included George T. Downing who was a pioneer youth leader and later an organizer of several black regiments of soldiers in New York City. David Ruggles was one of the first blacks to escape from slavery and later published the first magazine edited by a black. Also, Henry Highland Garnet, pastor of a white church in Troy, New York was a militant black who publicly incited slaves to revolt against their masters.

# CHAPTER II

## Antebellum Slavery

*Oh, could slavery exist long*
*if it did not sit on a commercial throne?*
Frances Ellen Watkin Harper-1854

In 1840 the American slave system seemed secure to many people. The abolitionists were still agitating, but the last of the great slave uprisings in the South under Nat Turner had been thoroughly repressed. After the 1831 Nat Turner insurrection, no serious outbreaks occurred as the slave states strengthened their patrol and militia defenses, passed more stringent slave codes, closed ranks, and permitted no criticism at home of the institution of slavery.

The type of slavery established in the United States was unusual in form and has been labeled by one revisionist historian as "the peculiar institution." The slave was looked upon as his master's property for life, and unlike the slavery of antiquity there were no gradual or automatic provisions for manumission. Slaves had no rights and family ties were not respected. Husbands, wives, and children were often separated and sold at the master's whim. Under these conditions no group of people could be content and blacks were no exception. However, unlike Native Americans who were so militant to white oppression that it threatened them to near extinction, blacks ostensibly succumbed to slavery's brute force. Also unlike Native Americans, whose nomadic warrior heritage and fighting spirit made them difficult to control in slavery, blacks reacted differently for purposes of survival.

The happy, content, and humble appearance of the slave was a guise, a role which was played to serve his best interests but when examined proved to be false. This guise served to subdue many white reactions to the slave's day-to-day protest. The slave was extremely cautious when talking to whites and he was a "yes man" par excellence. By the intonations of his master's voice, the slave had come to know what kind of response the master wanted. To the slave, the truth or falsity of what he said was unimportant compared to saying what the master wanted to hear.

Decades after emancipation this guise would feed the inferior stereotype set in the minds of many white Americans. So successful was the slave in acting out this role of survival, psychologists a hundred years later posed the question as to whether the behavior pattern had become internalized -- that the mask had become the man, that the Sambo stereotype had become a true Sambo. The stereotype of blacks being happy, humble creatures would prove to be highly appropriate for the citizen second-class status that was subsequently consigned to them.

In 1850 the South solidified its position on slavery by wrangling from Congress The Fugitive Slave Act. This meant that all Americans, under pain of fine or imprisonment, were compelled to assist in the capture of fugitive slaves. The Fugitive Slave Act was compared to the Stamp Act of 1765 which sowed the seeds of discontent leading to the American Revolutionary War. Charles Sumner, the notable abolitionist senator from Massachusetts, stated that the Act was disowned and discredited within a year of its passage, and that it violated the Constitution and "so shocked the public conscience that all honest men were bound to disobey it" (Tyler, 1944). However, the South partially staked its future allegiance to the Union on the enforcement of this Act and it was viewed as

Slaves were driven westward as new land was sought on the frontier. (Photo courtesy of William L. Katz Collection.)

southern economic security. The increased importance of cotton in the South also strengthened the hold of slavery as the price of a black prime field hand tripled in a thirty-year period.

## The Slave Types

Basically, there were three types of slaves in America: town slaves, house slaves, and field slaves. Town slaves were usually better off because the master-slave relationship was at its weakest in urban life. Some towns had a population which consisted of 37 percent slaves. Town masters knew that if their skilled slaves were to be employed they had to have permission to go out and make their own arrangements. Town slave families generally lived in small, windowless quarters in back of the master's house which comprised an enclosure of high walls that constantly reminded them of servitude. When more than one slave was needed in the household, the master brought in others and a haphazard mating between the sexes resulted in a "family" after a few years. However, the age range among the slaves thrown together under these conditions was often dysfunctional. Also, the relationships between the slaves were so vague that familial stability was rarely achieved. This elevated and accentuated the role of the slave mother in the towns and Wade (1965) contends that:

> To the extent that there was a family center, she was it. Her spouse came to visit her, shared her room, even took her ("Mary's Alfred") name. Except for the sexual relation, this union bore little resemblance to the marriage institution that whites understood (p.119).

In many instances self-hire was a stepping stone to self-purchase. Town slaves mingled with free blacks in church and at social affairs, and had some contact with urban life. Consequently, they carried themselves with an air of assurance not seen in their rural brothers. Whites often complained publicly about the "insolence and insubordination" of town slaves. Slavery was not conducive to a dense population where there was a majority of non-slaveholders. Only one sixth of the southern white population benefitted from slavery, and these persons lived mostly on plantations and in rural sections. The sense of decency that pervaded most urban areas did much to check the outbreaks of atrocious slave cruelty openly perpetrated on the plantations. Town masters were careful not to shock the humanity of their non-slaveholding neighbors by inciting the cries of the lacerated slave, and very few in the towns were willing to endure the reputation of being cruel masters.

House slaves were those who lived on the plantations and were given the domestic assignment of serving the master and his family. House slaves were often lighter in color because of illegitimate blood ties with the master, and by virtue of their being closer to the seat of power they looked down upon everyone except "quality whites." Many house slaves felt that they were far superior to other slaves and considered their jobs as a sort of family privilege to be handed down from generation to generation. House slaves as a group were the elite of the slave society because they were able to copy and mimic the slave master's culture more directly. Furthermore, the master systematically set this group against other slaves to suit his particular needs and purposes.

The black upper-class in the slave society was found among plantation domestics, slave drivers, mammies, butlers, cooks, housemaids, and coachmen. They dressed better than the field slaves, wearing uniforms or the discarded clothes of the master or the mistress. They ate better food, often the same as the slave master. They lived in proximity to the master's house and slept in beds, not pallets on the floor. The labor required of them was lighter and more congenial. It was the "mammy" who was often the confidante to the white mistress and sometimes had more than an intimate relationship with the master. Despite the benefits house slaves were subject to severe restrictions of movement.

Field slaves had a certain amount of freedom that was denied house slaves. This held true largely because of the open fields wherein they toiled for long hours each day. However, field slaves were subject to the total regimentation of the plantation which was a combination factory, village, and police precinct. They went to the fields in the morning and left their children in the plantation nurseries. Food was prepared in a communal kitchen and sent to the slaves in the field during the day while the evening meal was cooked in their individual cabins. The food was issued once a week and was generally coarse and lacking in variety. Most slaves supplemented this meager

The Fugitive Slave Law of 1850 caused a furor in many states but was enforced nationwide. (Photo courtesy of William L. Katz Collection.)

fare by trapping racoons and opossums in the fields, or by stealing from the master's supply house. Slaves considered it wrong to steal from each other, but it was considered right and proper to take anything that belonged to white people.

The field slaves lived in family type cabins and some in barracks literally alive with slaves of all ages, conditions, and sizes. The vast majority of slave cabins were dark, dank shacks built flat on the ground. Five or six crowded into one room with everything -- birth, sickness, sex, and death -- happening in that one room. It was the field slaves who were the more militant, and they revolted so often that it is nothing short of amazing that the myth of the "docile Negro" persists.

## The Plantation Sexual Syndrome

The strength of the black woman under the strain of American slavery is almost legendary. Not only did she have to silently bear the wanton sexual advances of undisciplined white men, she was also the object of blatant sexual promiscuity encouraged among black men. The black mother became the fountainhead of power in the slave cabins. Her half-white children and her children from one of several "roving" black fathers looked to her for decisions that were paramount in the black family. Some slave masters reinforced this feminine independence with their power and prestige, and they used it to suit their own purposes. However, the black mother was not exempt from the backbreaking toil of the fields. Frazier (1932) claims that as early as two or three weeks after delivery of her child she was required to go back in the fields to help produce the master's crop. Older, pre-puberty slave children were charged with the care of the new infants, and some assistance was given by an elderly grandmother who was too old or sick to work in the fields.

Many planters saw the folly in slave promiscuity from a practical, economical perspective and therefore encouraged slave family stability. While slave marriages and legal unions among slaves were explicitly denied under the legal codes, in some cases slave marriages were not only recognized but actually encouraged by planters as a means to discourage runaways. These planters promoted defacto ownership of slave dwellings and household goods, they enforced sanctions against adultery and divorce by using the threat of the lash, and they provided feasts and holidays for important slave family occasions (Fogel and Engerman, 1974).

Slave breeding was rampant throughout the South as there were sustained efforts to produce a maximum number of slave children. Despite slave apologist efforts of denial, there is ample evidence of breeding on the plantations (Bennett, 1962). Planters demanded that their female slaves (married or unmarried) have children. Many female slaves were sold off because they couldn't have children. Planters even offered inducements to promiscuous female slaves. The plantation sexual syndrome placed a premium on fertility with some female slaves beginning their families at the age of thirteen to have as many as fourteen or more children.

Stud farms, where virile young black men were housed and used to impregnate female slaves sent there for breeding purposes, were also used to increase the slave population. Substantial fortunes were founded on slave fecundity which saw a slave owner investing in a single girl, "putting her to stud," and before many years she had a family that was worth $10,000. Some slaves did not resist this system of permissive sexual promiscuity, but as time would tell it was socially destructive and would carry over into the sexual conduct and mores of future black generations.

The intrusion of the slave master was a common occurrence in the black family. All slaves were inculcated with the idea that the master ruled from God and that to question the divine-right-white theory was to incur the wrath of heaven. The exalted status of the master carried over into the legal realm since a slave's testimony against whites was inadmissable in a court of law, and severe punishment was decreed for harming a white person.

Few men of any ethnic group could remain uncorrupted with such awesome power, and most slave masters were no exception. While professing the monogamous tenets of Christianity, the corruptible slave master almost openly seduced and procured the cream of black womanhood in slavery to form a veritable harem while his white wife helplessly protested but stayed in her place in the "big house." The intrusion of the slave mas-

24

ter and his kind ranged from the kept black mistress who hoped that her half-white children would be set free in return for her sexual favors, to the outright rape of young black women whose fathers and husbands helplessly stood by in remorseful contempt (Blassingame, 1972). Furthermore, the half-white children resulting from these illegitimate unions were at the disposition of the slave master, and their allotment ranged from being freed at the master's death to being sold to the highest bidder thereafter.

## Slave Resistance

After 1831 the slaves resisted and protested mainly by fleeing to the North, sabotaging the slave master's crop, and working long extra hours to purchase their freedom. But the slave's primary form of day-to-day protest was intentional carelessness and malicious destruction. Subtle ways were invented to expend the energies of the master's realm such as feigning ignorance and feigning sickness. Stealing from white people became universal. Arson, poisoning, and robbery became so rampant that in some areas it became punishable by death. Self-maiming, suicide, and infanticide were committed as some slave mothers smothered their newborn children rather than to see them grow up in an oppressive slave system. Though none of these acts could be categorized as revolts, it showed that the slaves were anything but docile in the face of absolute power. They did everything possible to keep the system of slavery from being profitable, and in many areas they succeeded (Fogel and Engerman, 1974).

The manifestations of these acts of resistance and protest had just as much terrifying effect on the white population as did physical revolts. The threat or rumor of revolt was always present and there was a history of widespread fear of slave rebellion throughout the South. Southerners worried that the slaves would side with the French during the French and Indian War of 1754-1763; they worried that the slaves would side with the British during the American Revolutionary War of 1775-1783 and during the War of 1812 (some slaves did defect to fight for the British in the Revolutionary War); and the Louisiana Purchase was encouraged for fear of the contagious French philosophy of freedom, fraternity, and equality.

Territorial expansion also raised some legitimate concerns for slave owners. In the early 1800s Florida was annexed for fear of Spanish declared freedom, and at mid-century Texas was annexed because Mexico hated slavery. Local slave plots had an element of contagion and the relative increase in the ratio of blacks to whites helped to precipitate increased apprehensions. Indeed, the South became such an armed camp for fear of revolts that one marvels that more southerners did not become disillusioned with slavery to see that it was too big a price to pay for its bitter fruits. Mass hysteria was prevalent and southerners engaged in vicious acts of repression such as the mass hangings of slaves who only conspired to revolt.

## The Underground Railroad

After 1840 the main avenue to freedom was flight to the North by way of the Underground Railroad. Many of those who made their way deep into the South to aid slaves in their flight to freedom were blacks who were former fugitives themselves-- men and women who were willing to risk their lives to lead others out of slavery. They knew that the desire for freedom was in every slave. However, ignorance of the route to be taken and the means to be used, fear of the consequences of failure, and love for their families kept many slaves in a bondage from which they would gladly escape. Between Detroit and Niagara Falls there were little colonies of black fugitives who were welcomed by the Canadian government. The Canadian government refused to return them and placed no restriction upon them other than those common to all settlers.

The Underground Railroad was an organized movement that consisted of a loosely knit network of stations, located a day's journey apart, which were used to receive slave fugitives assisted by persons known as conductors. The conductors were not only northern blacks and whites, they also included southern whites who held strategic, valuable positions on the Underground Railroad. Levi Coffin, a white Quaker in Cincinnati, was so successful in helping slave fugitives that he was sometimes referred to as the "President of the Underground Railroad." In his operations he employed free blacks who owned no property and who could lose nothing if caught by authorities who enforced The Fugitive Slave Act. The main goal of the

Harriet Tubman was frail and suffered from recurrent spells of dizziness but insisted on carrying her escaped slaves all the way to Canada via the Underground Railroad. (Photo courtesy of Atlanta University Center Archives.)

conductors was to re-settle the fugitives in Canada or in some safe place in the North.

Most of the operations of the Underground Railroad took place at night and during the day the fugitives were hidden in barns, the attics of homes, and other secret places. The conductors transferred their fugitives in covered wagons, closed carriages, and farm wagons especially equipped with closed compartments. Initially, the fugitives were black men but as slavery continued women and children also made a dash for freedom. According to Franklin (1974), nothing did more to intensify the strife between the North and the South than the Underground Railroad. Blacks and whites participated in it with a fanatical zeal that was systematically designed to wreak havoc upon the institution of slavery. It therefore put a tremendous strain on intersectional relationships. Southern planters looked upon the successful escape of one slave as a powerful threat to the entire slave community. Secrecy was the essence of success for the Underground Railroad. In both the North and the South its activities were illegal, and discovery was not only disastrous but expensive and even dangerous to its conductors and agents.

Primarily founded and run by free blacks, the Underground Railroad's most notable conductors were Harriet Tubman and William Still. Harriet Tubman, herself a fugitive slave, rescued more than 300 slaves and was considered to have been the most outstanding black conductor on the Underground Railroad. She knew many routes, many methods of escape, and many abolitionists of all walks of life. The New England intelligentsia as well as humble farmers in several states, North and South, sheltered her and her destitute companions.

Tubman was a daring conductor who had a price on her head of $40,000 dead or alive, and has been characterized in the South as the "Moses" of her people. She risked her life many times over by returning to the South to help runaway slaves to freedom. When slave fugitives became faint-hearted and wanted to return, she did not hesitate to level her pistol at the victim saying, "You go on or die" (Tyler, 1944, p. 535). Years later, Secretary of State William H. Seward made an abortive attempt to provide a government pension for her in recognition of her heroic deeds and dauntless courage for the cause of freedom.

Nearly half of the Underground Railroad conductors in the North were located in Ohio. The station at Oberlin College was one of the most important and five different routes converged on the town of Oberlin. The College was founded in 1833 and was among the first to admit black students. It was such a strong supporter of Underground Railroad activity that four times the Ohio legislature tried to repeal its charter (Katz, 1987). One of Oberlin College's graduates, Calvin Fairbanks, engaged in a regular business of transporting slaves across the Ohio River. He spent many years in jail for his conductor activities, but it was said that none of his slave fugitives was ever captured (Franklin, 1974).

.

# CHAPTER III

## The Social Impact of Slavery

*O, the length and breadth,*
*the height and depth,*
*the cruelty and the irony of prejudice*
*which can so belittle human nature.*
William G. Allen-1853

No geographic boundary separated the North and the South in their treatment of black people before 1860. Economics played the most important role in any distinctions that existed between the two areas, and slavery was a determining factor. The industrial North had no use for slavery and as a result its social stratum evolved more openly. The agricultural South felt that slavery was an economically sound method necessary to thrive in a fiercely competitive world trade. Therefore, its social stratum required all the rigors of a closed society designed to maintain order and supremacy over its slave population.

America's monomania, North and South, was its preoccupation with color consciousness. Although the North repudiated slavery, most northern whites thought as little of black people as did southern whites. The result was a singular social phenomenon where neither free blacks or slaves anywhere in the nation interacted with white people on a principle of equality or reciprocity. While the North hypocritically pressured the South to abolish slavery, there existed throughout the northern society a determined resolution to consider black people in all their varieties of color as beneath the dignity of human nature. In no respect were blacks worthy to be associated with, countenanced by, honored as, or so much as spoken to on terms of equality. Indeed, the social impact of slavery was not confined to the South, it permeated the entire nation because of America's pathological concern for skin color differences.

America's peculiar brand of slavery was largely responsible for its monomania of color consciousness. The institution of slavery in America evolved and was established at a time when the western Christian societies were making great strides in the scientific, political, and economic arenas of civilization. Subsequently, their military supremacy surpassed the rest of the world. Such strides were particularly apparent in the white Anglo-Saxon Protestant societies after 1600, and it was largely they who colonized America. It was almost a certainty that this group would feel that their technological superiority was synonymous with racial superiority over the rest of the world's people.

There were many reasons why blacks in bondage would fit into the plans of American colonists to help build the nation. The colonists tried many ways to solve their manpower shortage problem. They included inducements for the settlers, convict labor, and enslavement of Native Americans who proved to be unfit for slavery. But it was determined that African blacks were more suitable for the environment. African blacks, called "negroes" by the Spaniards, had already been successfully used in slavery in Latin America. That success was largely due to the hardiness of blacks under stressful conditions and the diversities in African culture -- though centuries old -- which fell easy prey to the invading slavers. However, the most significant reason was the ready identification of blacks among whites which served the purposes of containment.

In order to enforce their superiority, superficially based on skin color but in reality on technological advances of one culture over the other, whites developed many ways to make color the prime factor in any consideration of race relations. Out of this deception grew an avalanche of stereotypes reinforced continually by the color difference between black people and white people. The dilemma for black people was that eventually they could close the technological gap, but they would never be able to change the color of their skin. The dilemma for white people was that they had to either destroy the institution of slavery in its bud, or rigidly perpetuate a caste system that would facilitate it. They chose the latter, and color was henceforth utilized as a ready vehicle for any transitions or communications within the social structure.

Civilizations had known oppressive slavery before; some were also based upon skin color. But none had the socioeconomic ramifications and political overtones that characterized the American slave system. Bred in an era when reason, enlightenment, and literacy were beginning to be extended to the masses, American slavery found it necessary to implement stringent measures -- some physical, some psychological, some immoral -- to sustain white supremacy over black people. Consequently, the least humane of slavery systems developed in America.

The black family was severely undermined by the American slave system. White masters directed their violence, both psychological and physical, toward the adult black male and black emasculation was the order of the day. Even in biblical times the adult male slave retained some vestige of his manliness, but such was not the case in the United States. The black adult slave was made to cower and submit to the most inhuman treatment as his family helplessly stood by in horror and contempt. Black men were regarded as children and even called "boy" regardless of age. Into this family power vacuum stepped the black mother to serve as the family head. The result was a matrifocal black family where black children, particularly black boys, had more respect for the mother and very little for the father. The consequences of this sub-culture living amidst a white patrifocal family society proved to be devastating.

Although there were some free black men before 1860 who were able to take their traditional place as the family head, the vast majority of free black men, both North and South, experienced a similar emasculation in their role as quasi-citizens of the United States. Such emasculation destroyed the concept upon which families in the western Christian societies built their heritage and traditions. Furthermore, emancipation and the new caste system provided for blacks thereafter did very little to alter these conditions.

However debilitating, American slavery and its aftermath did not completely destroy the black family. Overcoming nearly impossible conditions of high mortality rates and economic deprivation, the black family made appropriate adjustments for survival. This survival attests to the resiliency of the human spirit, and it confirms the complex, compelling humanness of black people as displayed in American life.

Human history has shown that whenever man makes an attempt to contain life within a mold and to stifle change in a society, he makes change the more inevitable and the more violent. Such was the legacy of American slavery. The slave society was a reflection of America's peculiar social stratification which helped to split the nation into two camps: the North and the South. The abolition of slavery in America was cataclysmic and violent because the gap between the two camps -- as well as between blacks and whites -- had become so impassable and absolute. Indeed, short of civil war, it could not be bridged by any other means of transition or by any natural growth of human relations.

Such was not the case in the abolition of slavery in other parts of the world. In Latin America for example, blacks achieved legal equality slowly through manumission over centuries and after they had acquired an acceptable moral personality. In the United States blacks were freed suddenly and before the white community ascribed them a moral status. Since 1863 blacks have been struggling to obtain equal status. In the main they have found many whites stubborn in their resolve to keep African Americans in subservient roles. However, the field slave heritage of institutionalized ignorance and permissive sexual promiscuity has been equally debilitating.

# CHAPTER IV

## Black Christianity

> *. . . let American religion and wrong, American religion and cruelty, American religion and prostitution, American religion and piracy, American religion and murder, cold-blooded, and calculated by America's largest measure, shake hands.*
>
> Charles Lenox Redmond-1842

In antebellum America Christianity was the religion most often chosen and practiced by blacks, slave and free. This was greatly different from the 1780s when it was estimated that only 2 percent of the 757,208 black population was Christian. Newly transported African slaves initially rejected Christianity and clung to the religions of their African homeland which included the worship of one God with great reverance to their ancestors. They had difficulty in understanding a Christian brotherhood that condoned kidnaping people into slavery. However, with the institutionalization of slavery, blacks were encouraged to reject their ancient religions and to accept the faith practiced by their slave masters.

It is doubtful whether any people can fully impose their religion upon another by force or persuasion unless the recipients are ready to adopt the religion and to interpret it in terms of their own ethnic character. Unlike Native Americans, blacks accepted America's peculiar brand of Christianity in an ironic fashion. Although few white American Christians closely followed the examples, principles, and precepts of Jesus Christ in their relations with blacks, black people in and out of slavery overwhelmingly embraced Christianity. While sitting in the back pews and upper galleries of white churches, blacks caught the suggestion of the Christian doctrine. It was then adopted to meet their ethnic character and it was met with an enthusiastic and ready response. In short, black people subsequently began to "out-Christian" white Christians.

## Slave Evangelism

Prior to 1830 white churchmen in the United States debated about whether slaves should be christianized. But as great schisms began to occur among white Methodists, Baptists, and Presbyterians, southern white churchmen took a bold step in slave evangelism by concluding that prosletyzing the slaves would bring order and result in less slave insurrections. They reasoned that there was a missionary call from God to "save" their heathen slaves, that christianizing blacks was good for the welfare of the society, and that it would "civilize slavery in America forever." Although such rationalizations were self-serving and designed to placate the inordinate power of the planter class, white preachers in the South before 1860 began to make substantial inroads that influenced the development of Christianity among black people. Those inroads also contributed to the establishing of black churches in the South.

The Methodists took the lead in 1809 by establishing slave mission stations in South Carolina that were served by itinerant white preachers. The Baptists and Presbyterians joined this effort later. Most of these preachers had a home church with a white congregation and would contribute their spare time for instructing the slave populations nearby. They bartered with the planter class and postulated that no slaves well-instructed in Christianity ever revolted. Select portions of the *Holy Bible* were earmarked for the slaves, and by 1845 hundreds of mission stations were established all over the South where slaves were fully integrated into white church organizations. As a result, before the Civil War the Methodist and Baptist churches were the most integrated institutions in southern society (Roboteau, 1978).

The Baptists churches in the antebellum South had a total membership that was 33-50 percent black. Black people sat in the back pews or special sections of the church, they were called brother and sister alike, they attended integrated Sunday schools, and several black men became preachers in predominantly white congregations. Blacks adopted Christianity as a means to ease the pains of slavery, and white churches competed with each other to gain more slave converts. When the congregations became too large, some slaves elected to form their own churches. However, these black churches were usually accompanied by a white "overseer" who sat in the congregational meetings to insure that no sermons or activities were antagonistic to the white community.

White churches in the South were the greatest supporters of slavery and many white southern missionaries devoted their lives to the cause of converting slaves to Christianity. A prime example in this religious paradox can be seen in Charles Colcock Jones who became nationally known as "the apostle to the negro slaves." A rich aristocrat from Liberty County, Georgia and a Princeton graduate, Jones owned three plantations and 129 slaves. At the age of twenty-eight he began a lifelong missionary to convert slaves to Christianity. Although a staunch believer in slavery, he was sensitive to the plight of all southern blacks. He developed special sermons and essays for blacks and published a book in 1842 entitled: *The Religious Instruction of the Negroes in the United States.* He saw no end to slavery and was convinced that Christianity was the key for making it work in America. Although he developed palsy in 1850, he continued traveling and converting slaves in mission stations all over Georgia and South Carolina until his death in 1863.

Northern white Christians also proselytized the slaves. Refused by the planter class to enter the deep South, northern missionaries made more converts in the border states of Maryland, Delaware, and Kentucky. Large funds were solicited from liberal northerners and free blacks who viewed their contributions as a two-edged sword: one for the spread of Christianity, the other against slavery. These funds were turned over to selected mission stations and they became a foundation for the development and spread of black churches following the Civil War.

## The Black Church

Blacks, slave and free, copied the structure of white Methodist and Baptist churches. They gained experience in organization, leadership, and self-expression, and they re-interpreted the Gospel to the true meanings of Christian brotherly love. They also covertly fostered elements of agitation, insurrection, and disobedience. Moreover, they introduced hand-clapping and physical mobility into the liturgy, and Gospel/ spiritual songs were developed to reflect an appropriate meaning for their plight and desperate desires for freedom. Exemplary Gospel spirituals were: "Oh Freedom," "Go Down Moses," and "Steal Away," which represented a profound verbal expression of black other-worldly hopes and a speedy delivery from bondage.

In the antebellum period the black church was the broadest field available for black talent and the only sphere in which blacks could show initiative and executive ability. By the 1890s blacks had a higher average of church membership than whites, and blacks constituted one-fifth of the numerical strength of all the Protestant denominations. It was the consolation of religion that solaced and sustained the slaves under the heavy burden of oppression. Miller (1908) contends that had the slaves remained non-Christian there is little chance that emancipation would have come. He further states that:

> "It was the manifestation of the religious [Christian] spirit that gained for him [the blacks] the confidence and sympathy even of his oppressors and played no small part in effecting his emancipation" (Miller, 1908, p. 139).

The black preacher was much like a politician, and many secular black leaders began their public life as a minister. Frederick Douglass and Missippi Senator Hiram R. Revels were prime examples. Slave masters tolerated these men as a means to check the aggressiveness of their slave population. "Servants, obey your masters" was the order of the day and it was compatible with the bible scriptures that the masters deemed to be suitable for blacks. However, this policy of containment under the guise of Christianity did not always work as some black preachers used their pulpits, prestige, and positions to incite revolt.

Whites were often reminded that the most threatening revolts against slavery were led by black preachers: Nat Turner in Southampton County, Virginia in 1831; Demark Vessey in Charleston, South Carolina in 1822; and Gabriel Prosser in Henrico County, Virginia in 1800. Black ministers were therefore viewed with some apprehension. But the passiveness shown by black congregations during the period of 1840-1896 is strong indication that for the most part black preachers unwittingly succeeded in keeping black agitation to a minimum, and a "turn the other cheek" attitude among black congregations was the rule rather than the exception. Thus, white America's interpretation of Christianity greatly contributed to keeping blacks "in their place" during slavery as well as in their consolidation towards second-class citizenship.

After emancipation African American ministers were usually uneducated former slaves who, lacking entry to formal institutions of ministry, were "called to preach by God." The most obvious result of this emerging "invisible institution" after the Civil War was the rapid growth of the black church. This growth also resulted in the structuring of black family life to an extent that had not existed in the slavery years. The African clan and family had been decimated in the slave environment of the New World, and the development of a structured family life had always been nullified by the exigencies of the plantation system. Any concentrated efforts toward organization in the religious life of slaves or even spontaneous efforts toward their mutual aid on an organized basis had been prevented by whites in fear of slave insurrections. Organized religious life thus became the chief means by which a structured social life came into existence for black people.

The black Baptist and Methodist churches flourished because of their ecclesiastical independence from white congregations, and because they provided for a more emotional and ecstatic form of worship. It was not because of any peculiar theological tenets or administrative policy. Prominent among the Methodists was Daniel A. Payne of South Carolina who worked as an abolitionist as well as a minister. James F. Cook, a Presbyterian minister of note, helped to found a school for blacks in Washington, D.C. as church-schools were the only means for black education in the nation's capitol in the 1840s. By the 1890s the black Baptist and Methodist churches represented 90 percent of all black Protestants.

The work of black ministers, North and South, in establishing schools in the postbellum period was especially important since most states provided only a pittance of public funds for the education of black children. It was black men such as Payne and Cook, often with the help of funds from northern missionary societies, who laid the foundation for most of the black colleges in the South. Working with The Freedmen's Bureau which was created by an Act of Congress in 1865 to aid blacks in assuming the responsibilities of citizens, black ministers also laid the foundation for public schools for black children.

The schools and colleges established and maintained by the Protestant black church denominations between 1840-1896 did not attain a higher education level as learning institutions. They generally nurtured a narrow religious outlook and restricted the intellectual development of black students largely because of insufficient financial resources (Frazier, 1963). These conditions would dramatically change in the twentieth-century when black institutions began to reap the benefits of philanthropy and evolved to become reputable bodies of higher education.

The attitude of the Roman Catholic Church was in many ways parallel to that of the Protestant churches in that it did not attempt to influence political opinions on slavery. Some Catholic bishops owned slaves, but it was the consistent policy of the Catholic Church to impart spiritual knowledge to all slaves under their scope of influence. Black Catholics were few in the 1840-1896 period. James Augustine Healy of Macon, Georgia was the first black Catholic bishop in the United States. He spent many of his priesthood years in an Irish neighborhood in Boston, Massachusetts. Augustus Tolton, like Bishop Healy, had to travel to Europe to obtain admission into a Catholic seminary. Father Tolton became the pastor of St. Monica's Church in a heavily black population in Chicago and served there until his death.

The black church organizations began to censure unconventional and immoral sexual behavior that was encouraged under slavery, and further solidified moral support for a patrifocal family. Furthermore, it was in order to establish their own churches that African Americans first began to pool their economic resources to buy buildings and land in their communities.

After emancipation black congregations severed their relations with the white churches in the South. Blacks equated the severance as being congruent with their new freedom; whites generally said good riddance and saw the severance as a means to emphasize their preeminence in American culture and society. By that time two southern Christian perspectives had emerged: most blacks saw Christianity more directly through the *Holy Bible* with Jesus Christ noted as the Savior; most whites saw Christianity largely through theological disputes rising from the Protestant Reformation. American Christianity thus went full circle on a time table commensurate with race relations. In the antebellum years the churches were the most integrated institutions in America; by 1896 and into the twentieth century the churches became and remain today the most segregated institutions in America.

As segregation of the races in America's churches became institutionalized, white Christians continued their refusal to provide leadership and incentives that would dissipate conflict between the races. In fact, the primary reason for high church membership among blacks in the 1890s was a black response to the unmitigated violence visited upon them in that decade, largely from white southerners who called themselves Christians (Du Bois, 1903).

Whites viewed the postbellum black churches with condescending amusement. They didn't invade the black churches as long as the churches offered no threat to the white man's domination in both economic and social relations. But black Christianity in this period continued to be other-worldly in its outlook, dismissing the deprivations, sufferings, and injustices committed against blacks in this world as temporary and tran-

41

sient. Whatever failings the black churches had at this time, however, the important thing is that they gave blacks an opportunity for self-expression and status which they sorely needed. Moreover, the black churches served to develop morals and mores that had been sadly lacking due to the exigencies of the plantation system and its policies of permissive sexual promiscuity and black family destruction.

# CHAPTER V

## Blacks and Western Expansion

*. . . it was asserted that we are "a ragged set crying for liberty." I reply to it, the whites have so long and so loudly proclaimed the theme of equal rights and privileges that our souls have caught the flame, ragged as we are.*
*Maria W. Stewart-1832*

Western expansion in the United States during the nine-teenth-century was important to the survival of slavery. It also heavily impacted the status of free blacks, North and South. Expanding the nation's boundaries to the Pacific Ocean was called the "manifest destiny" in the 1800s as the number of states rose from twenty-six in 1840 to forty-five in 1896. How-ever adventurous "manifest destiny" may sound in modern times, in the 1840s the concept was synonymous with stealing vast amounts of land from Native Americans, the spreading of slavery in America, and the sharpening dichotomy between pro-slavery and anti-slavery forces. Mexico and its large provinces were among the first targets.

Mexico outlawed slavery in 1823 and in the early 1840s quarreled with slaveholders in its Texas province who wanted to re-install it. Slaveholders all over the South were firmly convinced that confining slavery within specific geographical

43

limits would spell its doom. Secretary of State John C. Calhoun even stated in a 1844 communique to the British envoy that the annexation of Texas was necessary to protect the institution of slavery in America. Hence, the Mexican-American War of 1846-1848 was waged to make slavery more secure under the guise of western expansion. Honorable men such as Abraham Lincoln, Frederick Douglass, and Horace Mann vigorously protested the morality of the War, but to no avail. Even General Ulysses S. Grant, who reluctantly fought its battles as a young lieutenant, later claimed that there was never a more wicked war than that waged by the United States against Mexico (Katz, 1987). The results of the War saw Texas, California, and land amounting to one-half of Mexico's national domain being handed over to the United States.

## Black Western Pioneers

Blacks came to western America as free men with the early Spanish explorers in the 1500s, they accompanied Sir Francis Drake to the San Francisco Bay area in 1579, and a small number had settled in California by the 1840s. Although they constituted only one percent of the California population, the largest portion were not slaves, and thousands of blacks participated in the Gold Rush of 1849. Many worked at mining gold and had their proportion of lucky strikes. These early black Californians usually arrived by sea and most, like their white counterparts, were easterners from New England who were simply seeking quick prosperity. Alexander Leidesdorff was a prime black example who in 1843 was one of the important business leaders and a central political figure in the city-state village of San Francisco (Lapp, 1977). Unlike Texas, the other major land taken from Mexico, California entered the Union as a free state in 1850.

Western expansion did not provide blacks a haven of freedom as it did for many whites, nor did the frontier environment offer much relief from northern and southern laws designed to constrain blacks. The "black laws" followed black people westward. Black settlers in the West often found their white neighbors clinging tenaciously to the folkways, mores, and legislation of the northern and southern states. As each western territory vied for statehood, the single most pressing issue

Nat Love, better known as "Deadwood Dick," a Tennessee slave who went West and became a cowpuncher, Indian fighter, and friend of Bat Masterson. (Photo courtesy of William L. Katz Collection.)

was the admission or status of the black population. Blacks were publicly resented by pro-slavery and anti-slavery sources, and as the rhetoric leading to the Civil War increased resentment of the black population increased proportionately. Several western states passed laws excluding blacks from entering their boundaries and Horace Greeley, the reformer who urged Americans to "go west, young man," made it clear that the slogan was meant for whites only.

Despite this hindrance blacks trickled into the West on a steady basis and in some decades they arrived in large numbers that threatened to bring an imbalance to the economy. The "Exodus of 1879," which saw a huge black migration to Kansas and other points west, brought a violent reaction from the white South. The fear of losing their cheap black source of labor to western expansion was a major concern to southern whites, and black leaders who acted as local agents for the "Exodusters" were denounced as troublemakers, driven out of town, or beaten in the streets. Congress even ordered a full-scale investigation of the Exodus. But after pages of testimony it was concluded that blacks were leaving the South primarily because of white oppression. Hence, oppression in the South spawned black western expansion, and by 1896 the black population increased by geometric proportions in the states of Montana, Idaho, Wyoming, Colorado, New Mexico, Arizona, Utah, and Nevada. The black population increased even more in the states of Washington, Oregon, California, Oklahoma, and Texas.

When cattle ranching helped spur the opening of the West, it followed that blacks would be in line for jobs in the lower socioeconomic levels. Cowboys were the lowest paid of these jobs, and many young blacks in this period moved westward in an attempt to escape the ideological turmoil between the North and the South. The black cowboy was no novelty on the Texas plains. Work was hard and the hours long with little reward except the freedom of the open spaces.

Blacks were prominent in opening the Chisholm Trail which linked the cattle industry with the northern consumption of beef. Many traditional western heroes and villains were black, such as Nat Love (Deadwood Dick) who was known for his outstanding skill in riding and marksmanship. When modern writers began to romanticize cowboys in books as well as

46

James P. Beckwourth, the most remarkable black explorer of the West who joined the Crow Indians, became a chief, and led them on numerous raids. (Photo courtesy of William L. Katz Collection.)

in movies, their racial identification was purposefully obscured to make the personalities more identifiable with white Americans.

Whenever a cattle drive was identified there were usually two or three blacks among the average work crew of about eleven men. Black cowboys herded cattle, served as wranglers and cooks, and sometimes served as the trail boss when the crew was entirely black. Most of the best known pioneer cattlemen had blacks working for them in some capacity, and they were largely recognized to be the most faithful ranch hands in the business. Blacks also worked as trainers, jockeys, and horsebreakers, and like their white counterparts, they did not obtain recognition unless they did something spectacular or disturbed the peace. Only a few of the black cowboys settled permanently in the northern ranges of Wyoming, Montana, Nebraska, and the Dakotas. Consequently, they are not well remembered or well noted by the twentieth-century residents of those states. Four of the more notable black characters of the West were James P. Beckwourth, Negro Abraham, Cherokee Bill, and Edwin P. McCabe.

As was noted in Chapter I, James P. Beckwourth was a black explorer from Virginia who discovered the Beckwourth Pass. In the 1840s he joined Dennis Kearney's forces in California and later participated in the Mexican-American War. Beckwourth participated in the gold rush to Colorado in 1859 and fought in the Cheyenne Wars of 1864. He was also a mountaineer, scout, and long time associate of the Crow Indians. The life of this black pioneer is exemplary of the multiple roles that blacks played in western expansion. Beckwourth's life and adventures were comparable to Kit Carson, Daniel Boone, and David Crockett, and he was considered to have been as tough a fighter the wilderness ever shaped. His exploits were so dramatic that Universal International Studio included them in the 1950 movie *Tomahawk*, but installed a white actor to play the role of Beckwourth.

Negro Abraham was a fugitive slave adopted by the Seminole Indians. As their spokesman in the period when the federal government was moving Native Americans from Florida across the Mississippi River to Oklahoma and Kansas, Abraham opposed the relocation. He feared that in the process of

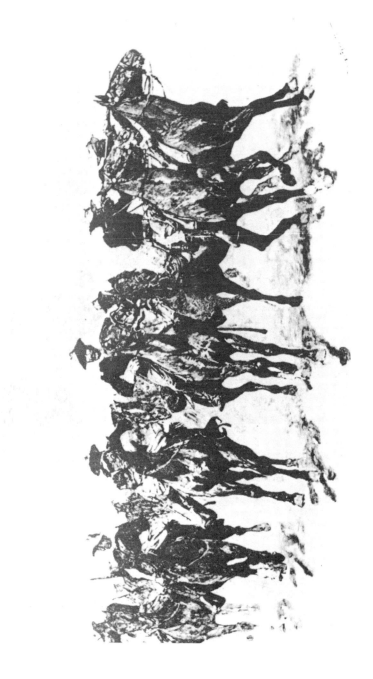

"Captain Dodge's Colored Troopers to the Rescue," a famous picture by Frederick Remington showing the Buffalo Soldiers riding against the Ute Indians at Milk River. (Photo courtesy of William L. Katz Collection.)

traveling through the southern states, many black fugitives under Seminole protection would be recaptured by their former masters. A diplomat of skill, he refused to accept the new site until he was assured of everyone's freedom. He also opposed settlement of the Seminoles with the Creek Indians because they were known to enslave blacks.

Cherokee Bill was the black counterpart of his contemporary, the famed Billy the Kid. His real name was Cranford Goldsby, the son of a Tenth Cavalry soldier, and he was born on the military reservation of Fort Concho, Texas. After his parents separated, he fell into bad company and had his first shoot-out at the age of 18. He became a scout for the Cherokee Indians and later for the Creeks and the Seminoles. He then joined an Oklahoma outlaw gang and began a life of crime. He was noted for his fast draw, he was pursued by women, and was feared by his enemies. Because of his association with the Native Americans, Cherokee Bill traveled throughout Oklahoma without fear of attack. Finally, he was captured and hanged in Fort Smith, Arkansas one month before his twentieth birthday (Katz 1987).

Edwin P. McCabe was the most popular black statesmen and the first to be elected to a major position in the West. Born in Troy, New York in 1850, he migrated to Kansas prior to the "Exodus of 1879" where he served as the state auditor for five years. He later moved to Oklahoma where he held similar positions, he founded the all black cities of Langston and Liberty, and led efforts to make Oklahoma a black state. But the black Oklahoma enclaves fell victim to white supremacy also, and "the black dream of Oklahoma became another southern nightmare" (Katz, 1987).

## The Buffalo Soldiers

Western expansion was largely facilitated by black men who served in the United States Army, notably the Ninth and Tenth Cavalry and also the Twenty-fourth and Twenty-fifth Infantry. Native Americans called these brave, fierce fighting black troopers "Buffalo Soldiers" because their wooly hair and dusty coats resembled a buffalo's mane. The name was not an insult to black troopers who were familiar with the great respect Native Americans had for the buffalo. The Ninth and Tenth Cavalry campaigned for twenty-four years on the Great Plains,

Frederick Remington's sketch of Buffalo Soldiers forming a skirmish line. (Photo courtesy of William L. Katz Collection.)

51

along the Rio Grande, in New Mexico, Arizona, Colorado, and in the Dakotas. They helped to bring law and order to the West by warring with Native Americans, bandits, cattle thieves, murderous gunmen, bootleggers, trespassers, and Mexican revolutionaries. They successfully fought under the worst of conditions which ranged from the broken, rugged, and torrid Big Bend of Texas to the rolling plains, badlands, and subfreezing temperatures of South Dakota (Leckie, 1967).

The Buffalo Soldiers were formed just after the Civil War as a segregated unit with all white officers, and they comprised 20 percent of the United States Cavalry in the West. They served to pacify the West and by twentieth-century standards may appear to have been black mercenaries hired by whites to crush red resistance to western expansion. However, the Buffalo Soldiers took pride in serving their country as free men in an age that viewed black men as either comic or dangerous. Army life, though rigidly segregated, thus afforded black men a dignity they could not expect in any civilian environment in the United States. Moreover, the Army provided decent clothes, discipline, and a skill development that most black men could not experience as civilians.

The Buffalo Soldiers fought with distinction and helped the United States Army win the Cheyenne War of 1867-1869, the Red River War of 1874-1875, the Apache Wars of 1875-1876, and the Sioux War of 1890-1891 (Savage, 1976). They became the most highly decorated group in United States military history with a total of twenty-four Congressional Medals of Honor and numerous citations. They served in the most isolated and lonely stations of the West where discipline was severe, the food was poor, recreation was nearly non-existent, and violent death was always near at hand.

The assignments given to the Buffalo Soldiers were not limited to fighting. They built many frontier posts and the foundation was laid for several cities such as Fort Sill and Lawton, Oklahoma. They scouted and located water, wood, and grass for eager white settlers. They provided support for local sheriffs and law enforcement agencies, and farmers and ranchers were made secure because of the Buffalo Soldier presence on the frontier. They also guarded stagecoaches, built roads, and protected survey parties.

Despite these notable deeds, the white population in the West generally despised the Buffalo Soldiers, and prejudice and discrimination often robbed them of simple justice. They were denied the respect due them as military forces, they were vilified in the press and in public discussion, and they often faced the hostility of the same settlers they were assigned to protect. Katz (1987) describes an incident typical of the times in Jacksboro, Texas where white cowpunchers enjoyed baiting black troopers on leave. When a white Texan murdered a black soldier and then killed the two black cavalry men who came to arrest him, an all white jury found him to be not guilty.

Although their white scouts sometimes included Kit Carson and Wild Bill Hickok, some white officers, including Major General George A. Custer, refused assignment to the Buffalo Soldiers. But others such as John J. Pershing, then a young Lieutenant, earned the nickname of "Black Jack" because of his successful ventures with the Tenth Cavalry. Paradoxically, the Buffalo Soldiers were often the cavalry sent to the rescue. In the Ghost Dance desperation of the 1890s, a portion of the Ninth Cavalry rode 100 miles to relieve Custer's famous Seventh Cavalry from a serious Native American encounter. The white company commander of the Buffalo Soldiers received the Congressional Medal of Honor for his actions (Katz, 1987).

The Buffalo Soldiers were first rate regiments and a major force in promoting peace for western expansion. They later served gallantly in the Spanish-American War and in World Wars I and II, and were integrated with the United States Armed forces in 1952.

# CHAPTER VI

## The Dred Scott Decision

*A community is democratic only*
*when the humblest and weakest person can enjoy*
*the highest civil, economic, and social rights*
*that the biggest and most powerful possess.*
A. Phillip Randolph-1942

The United States Supreme Court Dred Scott Decision of 1857 was one of the most controversial court rulings in the history of the United States. For over 100 years it has been prominently mentioned in American history and social studies classrooms, and for decades it was one of the few subjects that identified the plight of a specific black man in antebellum America. The Dred Scott Decision was important because it encouraged tens of thousands of white Americans to join forces with the abolitionists, it legally defined the status of black people in America, and it challenged congressional powers over slavery in the territories.

Dred Scott was a Missouri slave owned by a United States Army surgeon who on military assignments had carried Scott, his wife, and their two children to Illinois and the Minnesota

Dred Scott and his wife Harriet. Scott's master freed him two weeks after the Supreme Court Decision but he died soon afterward. (Photo courtesy of William L. Katz Collection.)

Territory where slavery was forbidden. Scott was persuaded by abolitionists in Missouri to sue for his freedom on the grounds that his residence in free territory made him a free man. But the Missouri state supreme court ruled against him. When Scott's owner died, his ownership was transferred to the widow's brother, J.F.A. Sanford who lived in New York. This expanded the case into the federal courts where it was to determine the future for Scott and his family. In the meantime, Scott and his family had run away to the Lucas swamps near St. Louis, a haven for runaway slaves. After saving 300 dollars as a down payment on his family's freedom, he offered it to his owner but was rejected. The legal battle ensued for nearly eleven years before a decision was made by the United States Supreme Court in 1857. Scott's freedom was denied by the Decision; however, the impact of the Decision precipitated a major crisis over the western expansion of slavery, it provided a volatile issue for the new Republican Party, and it subsequently helped to plunge the nation into civil war.

The Dred Scott Decision confirmed what the nation and most white Americans had been saying for over sixty years: Black people had no legal claims to American civil rights. Yet no measure by a branch of the federal government ever angered abolitionists and free blacks as did this Decision. The ruling permitted slavery in the territories, thereby strengthening it. As if that were not enough, the Decision also stripped blacks -- free as well as slave -- of their claim to citizenship. Further-more, southern leadership in the federal government which pre-cipitated the Decision made the outlook appear increasingly hopeless. Emancipation then seemed to be nothing but a wild, delusive idea. Also, whatever of conscientious scruple, reli-gious conviction, or public policy which had opposed the sys-tem of slavery in the past had subsided. In short, it seemed as though the abolition movement was dead.

Out of this despair and mourning of a lost cause came the words of Frederick Douglass in a speech delivered on May 4, 1857 before an abolitionist gathering. Douglass lambasted the Supreme Court and President James Buchanan for supporting the Decision. But he surprised his audience by saying that his hopes:

John Brown had a fierce sense of righteousness that fueled his extraordinary activities in the fight against slavery. (Library of Congress photo.)

". . . were never brighter than now. I have no fear that the National Conscience will be put to sleep by such an open, glaring, and scandalous issue of lies as that Decision is, and has been, over and over, shown to be" (Quarels, 1968, p. 60).

He further stated that such a Decision could not stand, and that abolitionists and black people should meet it in a cheerful spirit because it could possibly be the one necessary link in the chain of events preparatory to the downfall and complete overthrow of the slave system. Douglass further spoke of his faith in the United States Constitution and warned that God's justice would not sleep forever. Prophetically, he stated that if slavery is not eliminated, judgement more fierce and terrible would come.

Such words from the black leader who advocated non-violence were indicative of his prominent stature and depth of perception. The devotion that Douglass had for the United States Constitution in this time of crisis was significant. He viewed the Constitution as a means of assimilating black people into the mainstream of American culture, and his faith in it was reminiscent of the nation's founding fathers who wrote the Declaration of Independence. Douglass rallied the support of the abolitionists by his effective oratory and encouraged them to continue the fight for freedom despite the Dred Scott Decision.

The Died Scott Decision aggravated many white Americans, notably John Brown. A long-time fighter for human rights who had launched quasi-military raids against slavery in Kansas and Missouri, Brown in 1859 led a group of thirteen whites and five blacks to seize the federal arsenal at Harpers Ferry, Virginia. His intent was to spur a revolt among the slaves in Virginia. However, the slaves were too well contained, they did not revolt as Brown had expected, and he and his men were subdued by federal troops. Though Brown was hanged just six weeks later, he had ample time at his trial and in newspaper interviews to prick the conscience of the nation on the issue of slavery. His eloquence and death rendered him a martyr for the cause of abolition. Moreover, his condemnation of slavery had an electrifying effect on the North and the South that was as devastating as Abraham Lincoln's presidential election victory in 1860 (Franklin, 1974).

One may question the justice and morality of the majority opinion of the Dred Scott Decision, but not the evidence marshaled by Supreme Court Chief Justice Roger B. Taney. Taney argued that blacks in the United States were not citizens but property, and that blacks had no rights that a white person would respect. Moreover, Taney demonstrated that blacks had traditionally been excluded from full and equal participation in American life and institutions in all sections of the country. The Dred Scott Decision therefore ignominiously reflected America in the full bloom of human bondage.

# CHAPTER VII

## Blacks in the Civil War

*A government that can give liberty
in its constitution ought to have the power
to protect liberty in its administration.*
*Frederick Douglass-1888*

The fierce and terrible judgement that Frederick Douglass predicted in 1857 became a reality in the Civil War years of 1861-1865. The United States Civil War was one of the bloodiest conflicts in human history. More than 620,000 Americans perished on the battlefield. During the 1862 Battle of Shiloh in Tennessee, for example, more Americans were killed in just two days than were killed in the battles of all previous American wars combined. Some battles had staggering casualties as high as 30 percent (10 percent is considered excessive in most wartime battles), and the total American casualties of the Civil War were far more than the American casualties of World War I and World War II combined. Property losses in the South were extremely high, especially in Georgia, and practically no American family escaped from having a fatality or a wounded participant in the War. The nation thus paid a terrible price for

61

Black soldiers in the attack on Fort Wagner, South Carolina. (Photo courtesy of Atlanta University Center Archives.)

its inability to peaceably settle issues related to sectionalism, slavery, and the continuous hegemony of the Union.

## The Black Volunteers

When the Civil War broke out, free blacks at first volunteered their services to the Union only to be refused. The use of blacks as military laborers in the South brought a change to this Union policy. Free blacks responded with immediate enlistments and served under the designation of "United States Colored Troops" mostly under white officers. The fact that slaves from rebel states were welcomed to fight in the Union Army as free men served as an inducement for many to escape to the North. However, black soldiers were subjected to blatant discrimination and unfair treatment.

The most obvious slights to black soldiers were reduced pay and second-class service. Several proud black regiments chose to serve without pay in deference to serving at a rate less than that of white soldiers. The proud black Massachusetts Fifty-fourth Regiment served an entire year without pay as a protest against the discriminatory pay scales. However, when the Third South Carolina Regiment protested against the pay scales it was not tolerated. When they stacked their arms before their captain's tent "on the avowed ground that they were released from duty by the refusal of the government to fulfill its share of the contract," a company sergeant leading the protest was court martialed and shot (Franklin, 1974).

When the Union decided to accept black enlistments into the military, the issue of equal pay was widely debated. The military was prone to reflect the tenor of the times, and very few civilian occupations or work environments in the 1860s paid black men the same wages as white men. Consequently, pay scales during the initial stages of the Civil War for white enlisted men ranged from $13.00 to $21.00 per month according to rank. But all black enlisted men were paid only $7.00 per month regardless of rank (Cornish, 1970).

Despite the pay disparity between blacks and whites serving in the Union forces, black men volunteered for the military in comparatively large numbers. They recognized the Civil War as a fight for freedom, and they willingly left safe civilian jobs where even common laborers earned $15.00 to $20.00

The Fort Pillow Massacre where the Confederates executed 300 black soldiers who had surrendered. (Photo courtesy of Atlanta University Center Archives.)

per month. Many felt that black enlistments in the Union forces would have been substantially higher if Congress had not waited until near the end of the War in June 1864 to pay black soldiers at the same rate as white soldiers.

Black men served in the Union forces at far greater peril than others. When Confederate troops captured Union soldiers, black soldiers among them were rarely treated as prisoners of war. On April 12, 1864, Confederate troops captured Fort Pillow, Tennessee. Half the garrison consisted of black troops from the Massachusetts Fifty-fifth Regiment. The rebel soldiers ruthlessly murdered all of the 300 black soldiers who had surrendered (Lincoln, 1967).

James Lewis, a slave of New Orleans, is a good example of black leadership and courage during the Civil War. At the outbreak he served a Confederate officer for a few months and then became a steward on a Confederate troop transport. When federal troops occupied New Orleans, he abandoned the ship to answer the call for free blacks to enlist in the Union Army. Lewis was among the first to raise two companies of black soldiers who were former slaves. As Captain of the First Regiment of the Louisiana Native Guard, he led his command during the famous battle for Port Hudson, Louisiana.

Black troops had to patiently endure the persecuting hate of northern troops and civilians. Hooted at, jeered, and stoned in the streets of northern cities as they marched to the front to fight for the Union, scoffed at and abused by white troops under the flag of a common country, there was little of a consoling or inspiring nature in the experience of black Union soldiers. By the end of the war 200,000 blacks had served in the Union Army, more than 38,000 (19 percent) had given their lives, and several were awarded the Congressional Medal of Honor (Lincoln, 1967).

Free blacks had always served in the United States Navy, but after the Civil War broke out blacks flocked to this service to comprise one-fourth of the total Union Navy enlistments. Probably one of the most dramatic and widely publicized actions in which black seamen took part was the stealing of the Confederate ship "Planter." The ship sailed out of Charleston Harbor under the noses of Confederate guns and was piloted by

Robert Smalls (later a Congressman from South Carolina) and a crew of slaves. Smalls had engineered the plot and used it to deliver his family to freedom while he handed the ship over to the Union squadron that was blocking the harbor.

Blacks North and South figured heavily in the Union's successful effort despite the fact that initially their services were not welcomed. Black soldiers fought valiantly as their casualties were 40 percent higher than those of white soldiers. For example, the Fifth United States Colored Heavy Artillery lost 829 men, the largest number of losses in the Union Army (Franklin, 1974). Black soldiers proved to be brave and competent fighting men. Some were draft replacements, blacks legally paid by whites to serve in their place in the Union Army.

## The Port Royal Experiment

The First and Second South Carolina Volunteers were black regiments established near the beginning of the Civil War which became part of an important activity called "The Port Royal Experiment." These regiments, along with the Louisiana Native Guard, were among the first to contain slaves that fought for the Union. When the Union forces captured Port Royal, South Carolina in November 1861, the white population fled and left 10,000 slaves who had worked the lucrative cotton plantations located in the South Carolina Sea Islands just south of Charleston. After federal agents arrived to collect what was a bumper crop for that year, the question was raised about the consignment of the black population who were no longer slaves but who were not yet free. Northern abolitionists and philanthropists, aided by anti-slavery sources and the Union government, decided to conduct an experiment where the slaves would be freed and continue working on the plantations for wages (Pearson, 1969). A great deal of publicity was given to the experiment and many northerners kept up with its progress through a regular coverage by newspaper reporters.

In the Spring of 1862, abolitionist teachers and labor superintendents descended upon Port Royal from Boston, New York, and Philadelphia. These mostly young men and women were called "Gideonites," they were paid $25 to $50 per month by special educational commissions set up in the North, and they set social and political precedents which later spread throughout the South when the Emancipation Proclamation was consummated. They established schools for blacks, introduced them to democratic political processes, and transformed them into freedmen, soldiers, and citizens. It was in many ways "a dress rehearsal for Reconstruction," and some abolitionists saw it as an opportunity to demonstrate that blacks could function as free people. The Port Royal Experiment was the first realistic, practical pursuit of the American Dream for black people. For the first time in America, a slave labor economy was converted into free enterprise where black people could work for wages. It also produced a cadre of black soldiers who fought bravely for the Union.

The First and Second South Carolina Volunteers were not entirely voluntary enlistments. Major General David Hunter, who was the Commander of the South, issued a draft notice on May 12, 1862 that also included a "military emancipation" of the Sea Island slaves. The draft called for all able-bodied black men between the ages of eighteen and forty-five to be immediately sent to Hilton Head Island for military service. Both edicts were later revoked by President Abraham Lincoln. Moreover, the Gideonites resented the draft because it took men away from the economic structure they were re-building to help the newly freed slaves. Hunter, who was a staunch abolitionist, was convinced that black men could demonstrate their capacity for freedom only through military participation. The issue was settled when Major General Rufus Saxton, also an abolitionist and the Military Governor of the Sea Islands, set forth procedures to encourage black volunteers from several coastal areas including Georgia and Florida. Saxton's approach was more in tune with what the Union authorities would allow and it set the stage for establishing the First South Carolina Volunteers.

The First South Carolina Volunteers, commanded by Colonel Thomas Wentworth Higginson, gained fame for their raids in coastal Confederate held territories. These raids captured valuable supplies of lumber, bricks, and iron which were badly needed by the Union forces. The raids also were used as a means of recruiting more black fighting men. Higginson, an abolitionist from Boston, reported that his recruits were very docile and childlike toward the Union officers, but in combat they went through an "amazing transformation" to become

67

fierce warriors of the highest caliber whose knowledge of the local terrain made them a formidable foe. Higginson was deeply sympathetic to blacks and their religion and referred to his men as "a Gospel Army" (Rose, 1964). He was also a scholar who years later wrote vivid accounts of his army life with black troops ( Higginson, 1962).

The Second South Carolina Volunteers gained a different fame as they were commanded by Colonel James Montgomery. An abolitionist like Higginson, Montgomery had been a guerilla fighter in Kansas with John Brown, he had made his reputation as a plunderer with the Third Kansas Volunteers, and he was influenced by Browns' military tactics. Under his command, the Second South Carolina Volunteers brought the Civil War to the civilian population with massive raids and assaults on Confederate property. Like General William T. Sherman, Montgomery engaged in a scorched-earth effort to inject an element of terror on the coastal areas, and his raids were marked by excessive vandalism. For a short time after their arrival, the Massachusetts Fifty-fourth Regiment was brigaded under Montgomery. He also reinstalled the forcible drafting of black freedmen, many of whom were old men and invalids not fit for military service. Union authorities began to regard the Sea Islands as an inexhaustible source of black manpower, and they authorized bounties for the impressment of black men into military service. As a third regiment of black troops in South Carolina was being formed for service, the military aspect of the Port Royal Experiment had mixed results. Black soldiers in South Carolina made substantial contributions to the Union war effort, but they were also the victims of draft exploitation from ruthless northern carpetbaggers.

The Gideonites showed great courage in the Port Royal Experiment. They left comfortable, safe homes in the North to find the Sea Islands an inhospitable place to do "anti-slavery work." But the opportunities that gave substance to their dream of human equality were generated by policies of the Civil War, and they were ever mindful that the Confederate forces were just a few miles away. They were also keenly aware that if the Confederates regrouped to recapture the Sea Islands the Gideonite role as protectors and educators of slaves would have been perceived as seditious insurrection. During the Civil War, several hundred Gideonites arrived on the Sea Islands and they were divided along sectarian lines as well as their approaches to do "anti-slavery work." At Beaufort, South Carolina, the major town in the Union captured territory, the Gideonites often differed with the Union Forces as well as with their freedmen charges in their mission to combat slavery. The most extensive schools for blacks were established and a massive assault was made on black illiteracy. The freedmen began to take title of abandoned and confiscated lands, they participated in strikes and collective bargaining, and they began to participate in the political process to send delegates to the 1864 Republican Convention. However, the delegates were not seated on the grounds that South Carolina had not yet rejoined the Union. Some Gideonites were selfish men who exploited the freedmen, but all contributed to The Port Royal Experiment which was a training ground for postwar Reconstruction and a demonstration that free enterprise was less costly than slavery. That notion was not universally accepted by white people in Civil War America.

## The Massachusetts 54th Regiment

The Massachusetts Fifty-fourth Regiment was the first black regiment recruited and trained in the North. In an age where state governors were given the authority to form fighting units, Massachusetts Governor John Albion Andrew was authorized by the Secretary of War to raise an infantry which included volunteers of African decent. Governor Andrew was a staunch abolitionist who had financially supported John Brown, and he was anxious to engage black troops on the side of the Union. However, most whites even in Massachusetts doubted that black men would fight and others shuddered at the thought of armed black men assembled for any reason.

It was determined that 25-year-old Robert Gould Shaw would lead the Massachusetts Fifty-fourth Regiment. Shaw was a rich white Bostonian whose father was an abolitionist friend of Governor Andrew, and he was a veteran soldier who had been wounded in a Civil War battle. Shaw was a man drawn to difficult tasks, he soon proved to be worthy of his assignment, and he earned the respect of his black troops. It was also determined that the Regiment would have only young white officers who would be above a "vulgar contempt for color." Boston blacks were disappointed that black officers would not be engaged; however, Frederick Douglas and other black leaders assured them that "half a loaf would be better than none."

Recruitment for the Massachusetts Fifty-fourth Regiment first began in Boston, the center of the anti-slavery movement. Nearly half of Boston's black population in the 1860s lived on four streets where a small but well organized group of poor free-born blacks and ex-slaves bunched together for purposes of protection. They were strictly segregated and were often the targets of frustrated Irish immigrants who themselves were the brunt of vicious acts of bigotry and discrimination from the general population. Black Bostonians militantly defended slave runaways despite the continued intrusion of roving white slave catchers in their midst. They were among the most politically active blacks in the nation and they had more than their share of nationally known leaders. From the beginning of the Civil War, their leaders had unsuccessfully petitioned the federal government to allow blacks to fight for the Union. When the call came for black volunteers in the Massachusetts Fifty-fourth Regiment, Boston blacks were among the first to apply. New Bedford, Massachusetts was also a fertile ground for recruitments.

Governor Andrew had hoped to form a regiment containing only black men from Massachusetts; however, it was determined that the black population in that state was not large enough to produce the 1,000 men needed to fill a regiment. Many whites felt that such numbers could not be recruited among blacks in the entire North, and others were convinced that black men would not volunteer to fight for the Union cause. The Regiment recruiters took a different stance to portray the Union cause as a fight for black freedom, and they successfully recruited in several northern states. The most prominent black abolitionists were hired as recruiters. Frederick Douglass recruited in New York and Pennsylvania; Martin R. Delaney, who was a leading black physician in Pennsylvania, recruited in the Midwest; and John Sweat, who was a black dentist, physician, and lawyer in Boston, recruited in the New England states. Douglass was one of the most effective recruiters who at one Boston rally proclaimed:

70

"We can get at the throat of treason and slavery through the State of Massachusetts. She was first in the War of Independence; first to break the chains of her slaves; first to make the black man equal before the law; first to admit colored children to her common schools. She was the first to answer with her blood the alarm-cry of the nation when its capitol was menaced by the Rebels. You know her patriotic Governor, and you know Charles Summer. I need add no more. Massachusetts now welcomes you as her soldiers." (Burchard, 1965 p. 79.)

White recruiters were also used, the most prominent of which was George L. Stearns. Stearns was a wealthy abolitionist, a protegé of Governor Andrew, and a financial supporter of John Brown's raid at Harpers Ferry, Virginia. He traveled extensively in the Midwest and in Canada to recruit blacks at his own expense. He also was the subject of great ridicule from the press and threats from some whites who were unsympathetic to the formation of black troops. The fervor which Stearns put into the recruitment of black troops reflected the excitement that the Massachusetts Fifty-fourth Regiment created among the abolitionists. For years the abolitionists had labored in vain to destroy slavery, they were convinced that an opportunity for its death nell had at last arrived, and they were determined to take advantage of it. Recruitment standards were purposefully set higher in attempts to establish a black regiment that could excel in the face public scrutiny. The result was the formation of a regiment of men who were probably better educated and more physically fit than any other Union troops in the nation.

Public reaction to black recruitment was apprehensive in that many northern whites continued to express strong reservations for the formation of a black regiment. However, there had been a sharp decline in the number of white enlistments for the Union, the War had not ended as soon as many expected, and the Lincoln administration had begun to use the Confiscation Act of 1862 to draft persons into the armed services. Despite the unpopularity of the draft, northern whites did not initially view the formation of black troops as a suitable alternative. Recruitment of blacks in some cities had to take place in secrecy for fear of white mob violence. The apprehensions were so great in Philadelphia that black recruits had to be assembled in small groups under the cover of darkness in order to be transported to Boston for training. Nevertheless, the cream of black manhood in the North was subsequently recruited, and it included Martin R. Delaney's son, two sons of Frederick Douglass, and the grandson of Sojourner Truth.

The Massachusetts Fifty-fourth Regiment was filled by the Spring of 1863 and the new troops were assembled in Camp Meigs just south of Boston. Their training was a matter of great interest and a center of attraction for northern whites who doubted that blacks had the intelligence to master the complicated military drills that were prevalent and necessary for nineteenth-century infantry warfare. Within a few weeks, the black troops proved to be worthy of their charge, and on Sunday afternoons a large contingent of Bostonians would regularly visit Camp Meigs just to see the new Regiment go through their daily drills. By May 1863 the Regiment had demonstrated military preparations to fight. Colonel Robert Shaw was so proud of his black troops that he wanted to march them South through New York and through other urban areas on the way to the battle front. He posited that this would encourage black recruitments along the way; however, it was determined that such a show of force with black men would be confrontational to northern white racists. When they set sail for South Carolina on May 28, 1863, the Massachusetts Fifty-fourth Regiment had set the stage for 20 other northern black regiments that were being formed to follow in their footsteps.

The Massachusetts Fifty-fourth Regiment arrived in the Sea Islands of South Carolina where the Union forces had established a foothold. They were to be engaged in several battles during the Civil War, but the most famous was the attack at Fort Wagner on Morris Island which was part of the attempt to take the city of Charleston, the citadel of the Confederacy. After marching two days and two nights without food or sleep, the Massachusetts Fifty-fourth Regiment was assigned the task of leading the charge up the slopes of Fort Wagner, one of the strongest earthworks ever built. Although they were accompanied by white Union troops, the charge was unsuccessful and the casualties were extremely high, including the death of Colonel Robert Shaw. However, the bravery shown by the black troops impressed even the Confederate forces, their fame spread throughout the Union Army, and it gave public assurances that black men would fight as tenaciously as white men for the cause of the Union. Several months later, Charleston did fall and the Massachusetts Fifty-fourth Regiment was at the forefront of troops who marched in as conquerors.

William Harvey Carney was one of the heroes of the Massachusetts Fifty-fourth Regiment and was the first black soldier to be awarded the Congressional Medal of Honor. Carney was born a slave in Norfolk, Virginia but at the age of 14 was freed at the death of his owner. His family moved to New Bedford, Massachusetts in 1856 in search of more freedom and opportunity. Carney was a very religious young man and seriously considered joining the ministry, but he joined the Massachusetts Fifty-fourth Regiment in 1863 to valiantly fight in the assault upon Fort Wagner. His heroism was not recognized with the Congressional Medal of Honor until 1900. During the Civil War, a total of 16 black soldiers (more than in any other American war) were awarded the Congressional Medal of Honor (The Negro Almanac, 1989).

## The Southern Home Front

On the southern home front it became crystal clear by January, 1863 that slaves were making a substantial contribution to the Confederate war effort. Industry in the eleven southern states depended heavily upon black workers who were impressed by the Confederate Army as blacksmiths, harness makers, shoemakers, carpenters, wheelwrights, and miners. The need was also great for slaves in constructing fortifications and embattlements. On the plantation the slave was the stomach of the Confederacy, producing its crops -- potatoes, corn, peanuts, oats, barley, and wheat.

Confederate President Jefferson Davis wrote: "Much of our success was due to the much abused institution of African servitude" (Quarels, 1964). Davis contended that white men were able to bear arms by leaving to slaves the cultivation of the fields, the care of livestock, and the protection of women and children. Union General Ulysses S. Grant shared this opinion of the role of slaves and described the South as an immense military camp. Because slaves were required to work in the fields without regard to age or sex, Grant concluded that

hope that the President
my squeamish scruples of
g the Southern forts with
r that can be obtained

OF FREDERICKS-
RG.

we publish an illustration
's MAGNIFICENT CHARGE
FREDERICKSBURG, from a
ud. We have heretofore
battle, and will only sub-
count of the charge:
rebel position at Freder-
ed a number of times; it
fortress of the most formi-
guns were mounted along

ery member of the General's staff has been dis-
mounted. The brave Humphreys himself has two
horses shot under him. Here a strange thing oc-
curs. Howard's division, lying on the ground and
holding their position with the bayonet since their
ammunition was expended, opposes the advance
of the division of Humphreys. With pistol and
sword the officers threaten and prevent the passage
of another division over their prostrate lines, thereby throwing the advancing column into confusion
—a confusion which may have prevented this, the
last effort of the army, from being successful, for
through the smoke the rebels are seen running
from the wall.

"Humphreys's division has never been under
fire till this battle. But before that awful hurri-
cane of bullets no heroism can avail. The hill-
side appears to vomit forth fire, its leven glare
flashing through the fast-thickening obscurity

the cruelty of the scene. No help for the dying
patriots on that awful night. To attempt to reach
them was to share their fate. The murderous
traitors, without remorse, shot down all who approached. Men with children dependent on them
—men whose wives trembled for them—men who
had been little children, and whose mothers would
have feared to have a cold wind blow on them—
there they lay. Of no avail affection; not for
them the soothing touch, the warm chamber, and
the thousand nameless attentions of kinsfolk.
Drearily and with faint hope for the morrow,
tired, bleeding, dying, they must stay, their noble
efforts idly wasted in a fruitless struggle."

On page 28 we publish several pictures of the
Fredericksburg affair, from sketches by our special artist, Mr. Theodore R. Davis. One of these
represents GENERAL FRANKLIN'S GRAND DIVISION
RECROSSING THE RIVER AFTER THE BATTLE; an-

Butterfield sent an ord-
taneously Hooker ordere
batteries to the crest wi
fighting line all the day
centrate their fire upon
This was a perilous und-
most gallant manner.
through losing sixteen m-
fairly begun. Frank fel
to the left on the same li
with shell and solid shot
and seventy-five yards.
While their cannonade
head of Allabach's rese-
race, and was forming t-
the charge, and Tyler's
after, ready to support.
moved gallantly forward
fifty yards beyond, whe-
stone wall caused it to r-
forming under the cre-
pleteys and staff, and m-
mounted in this charge.
the brigade lost five hun-
Now there was but o-

REBEL NEGRO PICKETS AS SEEN THROUGH A FIELD-GLASS.

A *Harpers Weekly* print of January 10, 1863, showing black soldiers of the Confederacy on picket duty. (Photo courtesy of Atlanta University Center Archives.)

74

"the more than 4,000,000 of colored non-combatants were equal to more than three times their number in the North, age for age, sex for sex" (Quarels, 1964, p. 117).

As was suggested by Davis and Grant, support received from its slave population was a key factor in enabling the Confederacy to hold out for four years, despite the North's great superiority in manpower, supply, and material resources. However, the Civil War was fought mostly on southern soil and whenever northern troops drew near, the black population poured into their lines. Mass flights occurred as early as May 23, 1861 at Fortress Monroe, Virginia when commanding officer General Benjamin Butler refused to return slaves to their masters.

## The Northern Home Front

On the northern home front the civil authorities often blundered in affairs affecting race relations during the Union Civil War effort. The New York City draft riots of July 1863 was a prime example. The riots grew out of blatant efforts to protect the favored position of business over labor. Prices had soared while wages virtually remained stable. When black men began to be hired in jobs vacated by striking white workers who were drafted to fight for the Union, some in the white community perceived a conspiracy. The perception was that white men on strike for higher wages were being unduly selected for the draft (and replaced by black men) to fight in a war that would free more black men who would then take more white men's jobs. The perception was not entirely fallacious since an inordinate number of white men on strike continued to be drafted.

White mobs consisting mostly of Irish-American laborers went on a three day series of violent rampages. They burned down a black orphanage and wreaked havoc in the black neighborhoods. Union troops were called in to contain the rioters. Property losses were high and New York City Commissioner Thomas Acton estimated that 1,200 people were killed, many of whom were innocent blacks (McCague, 1968).

Blacks offered their services in city after city. They pledged their lives, fortunes, and prayers to the Civil War effort. Initially, the cities turned thumbs down upon this response. But as the War did not end in ninety days as some had expected, many whites changed their views about black participation to save the Union.

## Blacks and "the Great Emancipator"

President Abraham Lincoln issued the Emancipation Proclamation during the Civil War and has been noted by historians as "the Great Emancipator." However, Lincoln's conduct toward black people during the Civil War reflected the prevailing element of northern conservatism and racism. Frederick Douglass, who advised Lincoln during the War and was as close to him as any black man, later charged that Lincoln was no friend to black people. On April 14, 1876 he addressed a memorial crowd:

> "He [Lincoln] was preeminently the white man's President, entirely devoted to the welfare of white men. He was willing at any time during the first years of his administration to deny, postpone, and sacrifice the rights of humanity in the colored people to promote the welfare of the white people of this country" (Quarels, 1968, p. 72).

Lincoln favored sending all blacks back to Africa, consistently and privately spoke of blacks as inferiors, and professed a belief that slavery should continue if it meant a permanent breach in the Union. This stance was noted in the ill-fated colonization effort that he endorsed during the Civil War. He was informed that Haiti would permit two American promoters to resettle several hundred blacks from the United States on nearby Ile á Vache. The black colonists were promised a life of abundance but instead they were ruthlessly exploited. Half of them were dead within a year and Lincoln returned the survivors to the United States after he had discovered his error (Stampp, 1965). Lincoln was convinced that blacks could never become a part of the American mainstream because of the negative mind-set that white Americans held for blacks. Moreover, he did not feel compelled to change that mind-set.

On the other hand, it can be argued that Lincoln deserves the title of "the Great Emancipator." Although its original intent was to rile the South, the Emancipation Proclamation became an issue of great debate because it changed the character of the Civil War. No longer was the War perceived as only a fight to save the Union; it began to be perceived as a fight to liberate black people in America. Consequently, many northern whites withdrew their support for Lincoln, some Union troops and their officers were in open rebellion, and the opposing party in the 1864 presidential election campaign ran on a platform which included ending the War and retaining slavery.

Lincoln stood fast on emancipation in the light of strong indications that he would not be re-elected to the presidency if he did not revoke the Emancipation Proclamation. Lincoln proclaimed that blacks had fought and died for the Union, and to revoke the Emancipation Proclamation would be an immoral betrayal to their efforts. Subsequently, Union victories in Atlanta and elsewhere served to mitigate public opinion and Lincoln was re-elected despite his unpopular stance on emancipation.

## Churchmen and the War

Black churchmen in the North were solidly behind the Union and many black preachers served as recruiters for the Union Army. However, a lack of leadership among white churchmen, North and South, greatly contributed to the awesome carnage of the Civil War.

For decades white churchmen had debated on the "expansion of slavery" as well as the "retention of slavery." The expansion of slavery was a controversial issue in the white churches long before the engagement of forces in the Civil War. But the retention of slavery was never seriously threatened during the antebellum years. Slavery had been deliberately skirted by the nation's founding fathers in the 1780s because there was due concern that a compromise, essential for ratification of the Constitution and the establishment of the Union, would not be reached. Although a compromise was secured to form the original thirteen United States, the rift continued as churchmen joined politicians in espousing their views on slavery (Hill, 1980).

By the 1850s ideological conflicts increased between white northern and southern Christian leaders. As political sectionalism became more pronounced, Christian denominational differences on slavery produced even wider gulfs between northern and southern church congregations. White southern ministers preached fiery war-mongering sermons against abolitionism, they provided irrational interpretations of the *Holy Bible* for slavery's defense, and by 1860 most southern Christians were mentally prepared for a holy war dedicated to the expansion of slavery. Indeed, such was their fervor for conflict that even lower class white southerners who never owned slaves, who had no hopes for ever doing so, and who were ruthlessly exploited by the slave system, valiantly fought to the death for the expansion of slavery. And incorruptible men such as Robert E. Lee, who disliked slavery and disagreed with the Confederate succession, felt compelled to lead great armies in the field bent on dissolution of the Union.

Northern leadership faced an equally complex dilemma. Most northerners saw the need to end slavery but saw no place for blacks in American society. Many whites risked their lives and fortunes for the abolition of slavery, but even they were generally not prepared for a conflict that would result in equalizing the races. Furthermore, the white abolitionists were a renegade minority whose perceptions on slavery did not fully penetrate American Christian thought until many years after the Civil War.

White Christian leaders were unable to serve or chose not to serve as instruments of compromise between the North and the South. Many even urged that the two sides should fight to the death for their respective causes. Hence, by 1860 two white Christian Americas emerged: one North one South; both equally pious and God-fearing; one resolved not to condone slavery and the other convinced that they could not exist without it. The United States Civil War thus had many elements of a bloody religious war where, despite the claims of many historians who continue to debate the causes of the conflict, the pivotal issue was the indomitable presence of black people.

# CHAPTER VIII

## Black Reactions to Emancipation

*Locality, nationality, race, sex, religion*
*or social manner may differ, but the accord*
*of desire for civil liberty . . . is ever the same.*
*Mifflin Wistar Gibbs-1902*

The issuance of the Emancipation Proclamation by President Abraham Lincoln effective January 1, 1863 was accompanied by intense political persuasions. As early as 1861 Pennsylvania Congressman Thaddeus Stevens agitated and appealed for the edict, rallied support for it, and later bullied Lincoln into signing it (Meltzer, 1967). But Lincoln vacillated with a voluntary gradual emancipation plan that he felt was more suitable. As late as December 1862 he proposed that each state be allowed to develop its own gradual emancipation plan. Such plans would receive federal compensation and need not be completed before January 1900. States choosing not to complete a program of emancipation would not be pressed to do so and they would simply return the federal compensation.

Lincoln reasoned that his gradual plan would "spare both races from the evils of sudden derangement" (Stampp, 1965).

However, the conduct of the Civil War and the thrust for Union victories greatly altered his perspective and decisions. Hence, the Emancipation Proclamation was issued out of "military necessity" and it became the first step taken by the federal government to abolish slavery on a national level.

The abolition of slavery in the United States began with three edicts: (1) the April 1862 District of Columbia Emancipation , (2) the September 1862 preliminary Emancipation Proclamation, and (3) the January 1863 final Emancipation Proclamation. Congress enacted the District of Columbia Emancipation which freed the slaves in the District of Columbia. President Abraham Lincoln issued the preliminary and the final Emancipation Proclamations (identified as "the Emancipation Proclamation" after 1863) which freed the slaves in most areas held by the Confederacy.

All three edicts had serious limitations in their credibility. In efforts to placate the border states, Lincoln rationalized that he had no powers to free the slaves in those states. But at the same time his edicts presumed to free the slaves in the Confederacy where he indeed had no powers. Also, the edicts freed no slaves in the Union states, and the Confederate states refused to recognize the legality of the edicts. However, black reactions to these edicts largely contributed to conditions where institutionalized slavery would no longer continue anywhere in the nation.

Black reactions were threefold: a northern reaction with renewed affirmations to the Union's cause, a southern reaction of revolt mixed with paternalistic loyalty, and a military reaction which made a Union victory more certain.

## The Northern Reaction

The District of Columbia Emancipation passed by Congress in 1862 provoked the first black reactions to emancipation. Congress deliberated for months on the issue and Lincoln was encouraged to approve it by such prominent blacks as Frederick Douglass and Bishop Daniel A. Payne. When it became law on April 16, 1862, hundreds of slaves from the nearby states of Maryland and Virginia flocked into the nation's capitol to secure their freedom. Many of these slaves were later jailed by

United States marshals and returned to their owners as the Fugitive Slave Act of 1850 demanded.

Despite this perceived inconsistency on the part of the federal government, northern blacks felt that the District of Columbia Emancipation was the beginning of the end for slavery throughout the nation. There were no violent outbreaks or any attempts on the part of blacks to break down the barriers of social distinction between the races in the Union capitol. However, blacks in Washington, D.C. were convinced that the Civil War had generated the District of Columbia Emancipation, and they resolved to make the law profitable to their new employers. Some 3,000 slaves were freed by the District of Columbia Emancipation and it proved to be beneficial to slave owners as well as slaves. Much to the chagrin of black leaders, Congress also appropriated $1 million dollars for compensation to slave owners not to exceed $300 dollars per freed slave. Furthermore, at Lincoln's insistence, the bill provided for the removal and colonization of the freedmen to Africa. However, only a few blacks took advantage of the colonization provision.

The District of Columbia Emancipation did not affect the status of blacks in other northern cities. On September 2, 1862, the mayor of the city of Cincinnati, Ohio issued a proclamation calling forth all "citizens and aliens" of the city to assemble for the impending defense of the city. Recent defeats of Union troops in nearby Kentucky and a pro-Confederate raid earlier that summer had raised fears of a Confederate invasion. When free blacks reported along with the rest of the townsmen they were ridiculed and insulted by the authorities and told that their defense of the city was not wanted. The military authorities in Cincinnati had determined, however, to impress blacks for work upon the city's fortification. But blacks were denied the privilege of volunteering to defend the city, and the inference was clear that permission to volunteer would imply some freedom, dignity, or independent action of manhood.

Although Cincinnati's racial climate was an example of the extreme, it was indicative of public opinion in the North. Lincoln had to consider the ramifications of these conditions as he mulled over the issue of emancipation during the period between April 16 and September 22, 1862 (Brown, 1867).

Although most blacks were optimistic, the climate on September 22, 1862 for the preliminary Emancipation Proclamation was anything but favorable. During the following 100 days, the preliminary Emancipation Proclamation was the subject of serious and critical discussion on the part of most northern blacks. Many black intellectuals were disappointed because the preliminary Emancipation Proclamation was coldly indifferent to the moral and humanitarian aspects of slavery. But Frederick Douglass applauded Lincoln's move as one which spelled the end to border states influence concerning emancipation.

Other northern blacks in September 1862 lamented the preliminary Emancipation Proclamation's limitations in affecting only the slaves of states in rebellion against the Union. They were apprehensive that Lincoln, by virtue of the Congressional defeats he and the Republican Party suffered in the fall elections of 1862, would be forced to revoke the Proclamation. The election results clearly indicated that most of America was in no mood to continue the Civil War on behalf of freedom for black people.

As January 1, 1863 approached, northern blacks prepared a "Jubilee Celebration" in anticipation of the formal release of the final Emancipation Proclamation. In Boston, Massachusetts rejoicing throngs of free blacks met at Tremont Temple on the last night of December, 1862 for an all night vigil of songs and hymns of praise to God for the good news to come. The most auspicious speaker present was Frederick Douglass.

In New York City at Henry Highland Garnet's Shiloh Presbyterian Church, a similar all night celebration took place to host an overflowing crowd of blacks and whites. In Washington, D.C. a camp of newly freed slaves held a massive all night celebration. And so the pattern continued in almost every northern city and town. Speeches at these meetings extolled the virtues of Lincoln, damned the Confederate effort, and prodded blacks to continue working for the Union's cause. It was a night of celebrating on that Wednesday New Years Eve in 1862, a night in which few blacks in the North had time for sleeping.

The final Emancipation Proclamation went into effect on the following day January 1, 1863. In Washington, D.C. the District of Columbia Emancipation had been an uneasy emancipation because the Fugitive Slave Act was still enforced. The final Emancipation Proclamation had a national scope and was anxiously anticipated by black Washingtonians. A mass celebration was started on New Year's Day at noon and former slaves came out of hiding to join in praise of Lincoln's Proclamation. The unrestrained celebration in Washington was characterized by men squealing, women fainting, dogs barking, and whites and blacks shaking hands (Turner, 1913).

Blacks celebrated for a week in New York City with the largest celebration held at the Cooper Union on January 5, 1863. In Brooklyn Henry Ward Beecher, brother of Harriet Beecher Stowe, celebrated with blacks at Bridge Street Church and exclaimed, "the Proclamation may not free a single slave, but it gives liberty a moral recognition" (New York Times, Jan. 6, 1863).

The largest celebrations held anywhere were those in Boston. At the Music Hall in Boston, a galaxy of leading literary figures such as John Greenleaf Whittier, Henry Wadsworth Longfellow, Oliver Wendell Holmes, and many more joined blacks led by Frederick Douglass and Wendell Phillips in a massive tribute to Lincoln's Proclamation. Many praised Lincoln for his public abandonment of the colonization clause. For months blacks had tried to convince the president that the majority of blacks did not want to leave the United States. Since in the final Emancipation Proclamation Lincoln failed for the first time in public to mention colonization, blacks deduced that the president hoped to provide a place for them in this country.

In many northern cities, 100 gun salutes were fired and blacks throughout the Union praised Lincoln for his steadfast resolve to issue the Emancipation Proclamation while under immense pressure from pro-slavery northerners. For years thereafter, blacks all over the North and in some parts of the South celebrated the first day of January as "Emancipation Day." The slogan of the times was "Sixty-Three is the Jubilee."

## The Southern Reaction

In the South some areas such as Norfolk, Virginia, New Orleans, and Port Royal, South Carolina were in Union hands on January 1, 1863. This meant that slaves were not legally freed in these areas. However, one of the largest celebrations in the South was held in Norfolk. Blacks in Norfolk formed a procession and behind a band of drums and fifes paraded through the main streets of the city. This incident was an example of what happened to slavery when Union forces won control of an area. Slavery simply ceased to exist, the exceptions in the Emancipation Proclamation notwithstanding. In Port Royal blacks had begun to conduct themselves as freedmen when the Union forces took charge. For weeks they prepared for the celebration and when it came it was a festive occasion (New York Times, Jan. 6, 1863).

Blacks still under the yoke of the Confederacy reacted to the Emancipation Proclamation in a mixture of ways. The literate blacks read about it in newspapers and passed the word among the field hands. Some others overheard whites discussing it and injected it into the mysterious "grapevine telegraph" by which slaves passed along any news that came to their attention. Slaves were so well informed about the Proclamation by virtue of this grapevine that the New York Times was moved to remark:

"There is far more rapid and secret diffusing of intelligence and news throughout the plantations than was ever dreamed of in the North" (September 29, 1862).

There were many reports wherein southern blacks displayed the loyalty of little children when faced with the awesome prospect of freedom. A familiar story of the times recounted the black slave (with the slave master and other white men of the plantation gone to fight in the Civil War) enduring great suffering and ordeal in order to protect, feed, and shelter the white women and children left on the plantation. Laying past injustices aside and paying no heed to the Emancipation Proclamation which declared him free, the stereotyped loyal black slave labored on at the plantation and carried his load of work and responsibilities as well as some of those of the slave master. Typical and in line with these southern reports is the 1860s general view of blacks as a whole:

"The limited intelligence of the negro, the small brain and feeble (scarcely perceptible) reasoning faculties, . . . must be accompanied by corresponding domestic affections and an emotional nature that

84

accords with this limited intellectualism . . . . The strongest affection the negro nature is capable of feeling is love of his master, . . . who provides for him in old age and sickness" (Van Eurie, 1868).

A wide variety of slave reactions to the Emancipation Proclamation were reported as each observer saw blacks and drew conclusions concerning their actions. However, many observers judged without being acquainted with the backgrounds which influenced the attitudes and behavior of blacks in bondage. Some slaves were loyal to the Confederacy, especially those who were on intimate terms with their slave master's household and who had been well treated by their owners. But the great majority of slaves were field hands with no intimate ties with their owners.

White observers viewing slave reactions to the Emancipation Proclamation were prone to see the "faithful slave" as the southerner's literary antidote to abolitionist charges. They tended to paint a picture which justified the benevolence of slavery as an institution which ostensibly created a fellowship between blacks and whites despite the restraints occasioned by bondage. This view also facilitated the purpose of white supremacy in thought and action during the post-bellum period. On the other hand, black observers of slave reactions were inclined to give reports which salved the conscience and fears of northern and southern whites in the post-bellum period when a great deal of apprehension was expressed about the presence of black men in the company of white women and children. However, perceived black loyalty in the face of the Emancipation Proclamation goes against the grain of human behavior as well as documented evidence.

There is considerable evidence to substantiate that the thesis of slave loyalty was intended both for northern consumption and for the reassurance of a slave holding society constantly held prey by fears of slave insurrection. Even an analysis of the slave labor battalions in the Confederacy, far from substantiating the thesis of slave loyalty, actually demonstrates the contrary. Slaves built fortifications under the closest of armed supervision to discourage escape as well as insurrection. Also, the notorious "Twenty-Negro Law" of the Confederacy, wherein one white male to every twenty male slaves was kept at home, was regarded in many quarters as a necessary police provision to combat slave insurrections (Wish, 1938).

For generations black people in the South, slave as well as free, had lived under the most oppressive slave system the world has yet known. Slave resistance, though covert after the 1831 Nat Turner insurrection and ruthlessly repressed by whites in most cases, showed that blacks thirsted for freedom in every way imaginable. Hence, it is unrealistic to conclude that when emancipation did arrive -- by word of mouth or with the onslaught of Union forces -- blacks would overwhelmingly move to protect their white oppressors.

The facts show that blacks made a great deal of trouble for the Confederacy once the Emancipation Proclamation had been issued, despite laws passed in the South to repress revolts. They committed sabotage, espionage, arson, and assassination against their keepers. Slave insurrections, always a great fear and dread among whites during the antebellum period, became a greater threat after the Emancipation Proclamation. This threat affected the resistance of the Confederates who not only had to fight the Union from without, but also had to remain vigilant to the slaves within (Wish, 1938).

Insubordination, insolence, and disloyalty were common slave reactions during 1863. More than 100 black men were arrested in northern Texas when it was learned that they had planned to burn large segments of the territory and then escape to Mexico. Another mass insurrection plot was uncovered in Fort Worth with a white man leading the operation. Similar plots were uncovered resulting in hangings for slaves and white co-conspirators in Alabama, Georgia, Virginia, Missouri, and Mississippi (Wesley and Romero, 1967).

The fact that the Emancipation Proclamation provoked no general uprising in the South among the slaves can be attributed to three factors: (1) the close security system imposed by the Confederates in each state, (2) the psychological fear of retaliation among blacks (in 1800 and again in 1822 scores of blacks had been hanged for just talking about insurrection), and (3) the successful use of turncoat slaves to uncover insurrection plots. The general uprisings in the South that did take place were related to the advance of Union forces into a region. Slaves by the thousands poured over into the Union lines once they knew that they could escape the slave master's wrath. This was a problem of considerable note for the South.

A plan for a general insurrection throughout the entire South was uncovered by Confederate authorities who found a letter on a captured Union ship off the coast of North Carolina in May, 1863. The letter, dated May 12, 1863, was addressed to Major General Foster at Beaufort, North Carolina. It proposed that the slaves be aroused to damage railroad tracks, destroy telegraph lines, and burn trains and bridges. The insurrection was set to take place on August 1, 1863 and literate slaves were to pass the word to the field hands. The Confederate authorities, including General Robert E. Lee, North Carolina Governor Z. B. Vance, and President Jefferson Davis, agreed to withhold the letter from publication. However, warnings concerning the plot were issued to all Confederate generals in the field. Thus, the interception of the letter spoiled the element of surprise and the plot did not take place (Wesley and Romero, 1967).

Many of the slave revolts that came as a reaction to the Emancipation Proclamation were not made a part of immediate public information. Slave plots in every state were so contagious that they threatened to spread even further mass hysteria. Local leaders ruthlessly repressed the revolts, and then followed up with phenomenal procedures of effective censorship. The danger of inducing panic by spreading news of insurrections was particularly noted by southern leadership, and they recognized the need for silence at all costs. The southern leaders were fully aware that Lincoln's primary reasons for issuing the Emancipation Proclamation was to promote fear in the Confederate ranks, and they were careful not to oblige him or the Union war effort.

Another indicator of slave disloyalty concerning emancipation was the extreme security measures imposed after September 1862. The South, which for decades resembled an armed camp, had become even more alarmed at the thought of blacks roaming the streets as free men. In heavily black populated areas, many whites looked forward to January 1, 1863 as a day of impending doom. Although official Confederate reaction to the preliminary Emancipation Proclamation was general defiance, the Confederates buttressed their internal security forces

# Colored Men Attention!

## FREEDOM TO ALL, THE NATIONAL

## P O L I C Y,

## Now and Forever.

## SECOND REGIMENT KANSAS COLORED VOLUNTEERS.

———o———

BY order of Major General James G. Blunt, the undersigned is authorized to
RECRUIT ONE OR MORE COMPANIES
for the above regiment.

Able bodied men will receive $10 per month, clothing, subsistence and medical attendance from date of enlistment.

Hear what FREDERICK DOUGLASS says : "The decision of our destiny is now as never before in our own hands. We may lie low in the dust, despised and spit upon by every passer-by, or we may, like brave men, rise and unlock to ourselves the golden gates of a glorious future. *To hold back is to invite infamy upon ourselves, and upon our children.* The chance is now given us. We must improve it, or sink deeper than ever in the pit of social and political degradation, from which we have been struggling for years to extricate ourselves."

Recruiting Rendezvous—Office of Dr. Bowlby, Fifth Street, opposite Market House.

RICHARD J. HINTON,
1st Lieut. and Adjutant 1st Reg't Kan. Col'd Vols.
june19 d&wtf

Recruitment publicity in the July 17, 1863, issue
of the *Leavenworth Conservative.*

Recruitment publicity in the July 17, 1863 issue of the *Leavenworth Conservative.* (Photo courtesy of William L. Katz Collection.)

88

and strove to quell the rising apprehensions of its white population.

Some slaves simply refused to work after the Emancipation Proclamation reached their ears. But this occurred only in areas where Confederate authority was at its weakest. On Christmas Day 1862, the slaves of Magnolia Plantation in Mississippi, after hearing about the preliminary Emancipation Proclamation, decided to take the holiday off for a change. In February 1863 a Port Gibson white citizen complained to the Governor of Mississippi that blacks in his area were under no restraint and acting as they pleased. Hence, disorder and unfaithfulness on the part of southern blacks were far more common than post-bellum commentators have admitted (Wiley, 1965).

In the border states where the Emancipation Proclamation did not legally free any slaves, the black reaction was a paradox. Slaves in these states clearly did not follow the reasoning of the Emancipation Proclamation. They seemed to ignore the fact that they were not included, and began to act like freedmen. In Kentucky there were so many slaves asserting their freedom after the Proclamation that the *Louisville Journal* asked black Christian leaders to explain to the slaves that the Proclamation did not affect slavery in Kentucky (Quarles, 1953).

Whenever the word reached the border states, whether in Louisville or in Baltimore, blacks began to exercise some of the privileges of free people. In other slave areas not covered by the Emancipation Proclamation, such as in parts of Louisiana, planters became so apprehensive about slave reactions to the Proclamation that they prompted the local Union commander to issue an order advising slaves in loyal portions of the state to remain on the plantations.

Thus was the paradox for many slaves in Union held regions. They did not fully understand that the only slaves legally declared free were those still under the Confederacy, and that slaves in Union hands were still legally in bondage. They also failed to understand that their lives and destiny were caught up in a great struggle for state sovereignty, and that military solutions would be the final arbiter for their freedom and security in the United States.

# The Military Reaction

The Emancipation Proclamation was calculated to bring a military reaction that would turn the tide of the Civil War. Blacks, North and South, helped to make that calculation a reality by swelling the ranks of the Union forces. Its effects proved to be unnerving to the Confederate forces. Although Lincoln and the North hesitated to use blacks in the War effort, the Confederacy did not. Lincoln hoped that the Proclamation would sabotage efforts wherein southern blacks, free as well as slave, had strengthened Confederate forces.

As early as April 1861, slave-owning free blacks enlisted and were accepted in the Confederate forces in Tennessee, Florida, and Louisiana. In other parts of the South, slaves were impressed to build fortifications, and at the first Battle of Bull Run in August 1861 some loyal slaves were reported to have fought bravely by the sides of their Confederate masters (McPherson, 1965) (Wesley and Romero, 1967).

The Emancipation Proclamation had a section which provided for blacks to legally serve in the Union forces. But before 1863 Major General David Hunter had used black troops at Hilton Head, South Carolina; General James Lane of Kansas had formed two black regiments to fight rebel forces at Island Mounds in Bates County, Missouri; and other generals and state militia heads had accepted black enlistments. Although these actions were committed without federal sanction, Lincoln was encouraged and stated that he was impressed that blacks would so willingly fight for the Union.

The federal government chose a roster of well known black leaders to act as recruiting agents. Among these were Frederick Douglass, William Wells Brown, and Martin R. Delaney. Douglass' call to arms among young blacks emphasized that if the Emancipation Proclamation was made secure in a victory over the Confederacy by white men only, it would "lose half its luster." Douglass was convinced that black volunteers were essential to the cause of post-war freedom. His favorite appeal to black men was:

"Once let the black man get upon his person the brass letters, U.S.; let him get an eagle on his button, and a musket on his shoulder and bullets in his pocket, and there is no power on earth which can deny that he has earned the right to citizenship in the United States" (Quarels, 1968).

Northern blacks enthusiastically joined the Massachusetts Fifty-Fourth when the recruiting elements were firmly established. Black regiments were also formed in Rhode Island, New York, Connecticut, Michigan, Illinois, Iowa, and Kansas. The state of Pennsylvania refused to form a black regiment because of the resentment shown by some whites. But after the Gettysburg scare in the summer of 1863, whites became less hostile to the idea of a black army. Subsequently, ten full regiments were formed among blacks in that state. Ohio was also a late starter in forming a black regiment for similar reasons. Until November 1863 blacks in Ohio had to travel to other states in order to serve in the Union forces. Finally, after some difficulty in reaching the Ohio draft quota and repeated requests from black leaders, Governor David Todd began to recruit black troops (Quarels, 1953).

Northern blacks had not fared well economically before the Civil War's beginning. Systematically denied employment in most areas, blacks took jobs as "scabs" and strikebreakers which further earned them the enmity of white workers. By January 1863 the War effort had created a manpower shortage which provided job opportunities free blacks had not known before. Hence, some blacks in the North were not anxious to leave civilian life to join the Union forces at unequal pay once the Emancipation Proclamation gave them the opportunity.

The military reaction in the South saw freedmen join the Union forces whenever Confederate control collapsed in a region. Southerners, long accustomed to seeing blacks in subservient conditions, then had the culture shock of dealing with armed blacks on the side of the mortal enemy. The effect was just as Lincoln had hoped for, but blacks troops had to bear the consequences in the "no quarter" ruling of Confederates against blacks captured in battle. Subsequently, blacks fought in the fiercest battles of the War and they suffered the greatest percentage of casualties compared to any ethnic group. Their sacrifices heavily contributed to the success of the Union, and Lincoln, Ulysses S. Grant, and several Union leaders highly praised their efforts.

The Freedmen's Bureau tried to help blacks make a smoother transition from slavery to freedom and often served as an arbiter for black-white confrontations. (*Harpers Weekly* print in the Atlanta University Center Archives.)

The Emancipation Proclamation provided many challenges that were accepted by the Freedmen's Bureau which was created in 1865. Its primary purpose was to feed poor blacks, find them jobs, supply them with schools, and protect them in the courts. The Freedmen's Bureau also helped many poor whites who were similarly destitute and homeless after the Civil War. However, Congress made it an agency of the United States Army. It was thus authorized for only one year, and despite its best efforts it fell far short in dealing with the enormous problems facing black people in the South.

Black reactions to emancipation are documented accounts and concrete evidence that the Emancipation Proclamation did not "just happen" to black people. They were intimately involved with activities -- North and South -- which transferred a highly questionable, faintly supported edict proclaimed by an unpopular president into an ideal concept for freedom. This concept was accepted by the nation's majority as a foundation for civil liberties and was subsequently emulated throughout the free world. Had they not been so involved, black people would have had more difficulty in crossing the imperceptive barriers between slavery and freedom. Black reactions to emancipation thus served as catalysts for further legislation which assured that legalized slavery would cease to exist in the United States. Congress passed the Thirteenth Amendment in 1865 to make the emancipation of slaves a federal law, in 1868 the Fourteenth Amendment provided blacks United States citizenship, and in 1870 the Fifteenth Amendment gave blacks the right to vote.

The emancipation of slaves in the United States was an incident of magnitude second only to the American Declaration of Independence. It was in fact a revolution in the manners and morals of Americans. For the second time in less than 100 years the American people embarked upon a bold experiment that would affect the entire nation. Black reactions to the Emancipation Proclamation, coupled with a Union victory, assured that the experiment would have a fortuitous beginning.

# CHAPTER IX

## Black Enfranchisement

*Let us come together by the thousands from all parts*
*of this slave-holding nation and . . . kindle up the*
*sacred fires of liberty upon the alters of our hearts,*
*which shall never be extinguished*
*until the last slave of America is free.*

*Henry Bibb-1848*

At the end of the Civil War in 1865, African Americans played a prominent role in reconstructing the nation. In the North Reconstruction meant dissolution of the Union army and the building of various industrial empires based upon railroad expansion and the development of steel works. Although ruthlessly exploited along with white workers, blacks in the North were able to secure jobs as laborers at a rate undreamed of in the antebellum years. But in the South Reconstruction meant the rebuilding of physical structure, the rejuvenation of political and economic resources, and most importantly the development of a new social order where blacks could function as freedmen. With the assassination of President Abraham Lincoln in 1865 and no clear cut definition or interpretation of his Reconstruction strategy, blacks in the South faced precarious circumstances which first returned them to a status of quasi-slavery that was followed by a period of unprecedented black enfranchisement.

## The Black Codes

The former slaves as a whole felt a new pride in their country and a new sense of responsibility without the threat of the lash. But some folded their hands and waited for federal assistance at a level that never materialized and others wandered in search of lost relatives. Most freed slaves were resented by the southern populace whose world was in disarray among the chaos and confusion of defeat. Land reform was suggested as a means to assist the freedmen.

Land reform after the Civil War meant confiscating lands long held by the white planter class and dividing it into small plots to be distributed to the freedmen. In short, it meant taking land from whites and giving it to blacks. Frederick Douglass argued that such actions were necessary since the freedmen "were sent away empty handed, without money, without friends, and without a foot of land to stand upon." Prominent radical Republicans such as Pennsylvania Congressman Thaddeus Stevens, Massachusetts Senator Charles Sumner, and Indiana Congressman George W. Julian presented sound arguments for confiscating the land of "chief rebels" who were blamed for the Civil War and succession. But President Andrew Johnson, Lincoln's successor, sabotaged the successful efforts in land reform and moderate members of Congress blocked it because they viewed it as an attack on private property rights. Even William Lloyd Garrison, the famed abolitionist, was not sympathetic to land reform and the economic plight of the freedmen. Like most Americans, he felt that since blacks were freed their economic status should be determined by their own enterprise (Stampp, 1965).

Southern states, though Congress had not yet recognized them as functioning states in the Union, passed the Black Codes in the fall and winter of 1865-1866. The Black Codes were firmly endorsed by President Andrew Johnson. In reality, the Black Codes were designed to take the place of the defunct slave codes and the two had some features in common. The South Carolina code stipulated that in the making of contracts

96

"persons of color shall be known as servants and those with whom they contract shall be known as masters." Also in South Carolina, black farm workers could not leave the premises without permission. Vagrancy laws applied only to blacks, and they were fined if they had no lawful employment. Upon failure to pay the fine they were subject to be hired out by the local sheriff (Quarles, 1964).

A local ordinance in Louisiana required that every black be placed in the service of some white person or former owner who was to be held responsible for his conduct. In most instances, blacks were limited to occupations in farming and domestic services. Jim Crow regulations pervaded the Black Codes as Mississippi would not allow blacks to ride in first-class passenger cars, in Florida a black could be given thirty-nine lashes for introducing himself into any religious group or other assembly of white persons, and the ballot was denied blacks. In short, the Black Codes left blacks at the mercy of whites even more than the slave codes. The slave codes had given them at least the powerful voice of their slave master.

Southerners were surprised that there was a northern reaction to the Black Codes. Concurrently, northerners who had been sympathetic to the prostrate and defeated South were alarmed at the South's reinstitution of slavery under another name. Thus, southerners played into the hands of radical Republicans who were bent on extending their power into the South with the use of black votes.

## Radical Reconstruction

The Reconstruction Act of March 2, 1867 called the existing southern regimes illegal and gave the ballot to blacks as well as whites. The new black enfranchised were given assistance by white men who came south bent on an interest in political rule. Many of these Republican migrants were men of unquestioned honesty and ability, while others were plunderers whose goal was political gain and the quick dollar. The migrants were called carpetbaggers and they joined forces with southern whites (scalawags) who were sympathetic to blacks.

As black men began to exercise their right to vote, tremendous social changes began to take place in the South:

"Negroes and whites were going to school together, riding on street-cars together and cohabiting, in and out of wedlock (Negro men marrying white women in the South, but it was more fashionable, investigators reported, for white men to marry Negro women)." (Bennett, 1962, p. 184).

Black men suddenly became heads of their households and many black women submitted to this new authority with a great deal of trepidation. Some even drove their men away from home rather than to adjust to patrifocal norms usually seen in white families. Also, black men began to be elected to important political positions in the southern communities. They enthusiastically joined white northern Republicans and liberal white southern Democrats to reconstruct the South. This Radical Reconstruction was viewed as the fruits of the Union victory, and it looked for a while that democracy and national suffrage would become a reality in America.

## The Black Lawmakers

Assisted by the coalition of white northern Republicans and liberal white southern Democrats, the newly enfranchised African Americans were instrumental in bringing the southern states back into the Union. Although they were active in Republican politics the black lawmakers were never in control of any state legislatures. This held true even in South Carolina where for a time black legislators outnumbered whites by eighty-seven to sixty-nine. The total membership in nine of the constitutional conventions was 713 whites and 260 blacks (Quarels, 1964). This ratio of black representation could hardly verify the picture of "Negro dominated legislatures" so onerously painted by many white historians. Some blacks elected to state offices were both illiterate and incompetent, since it had been illegal to educate a slave. However, the overall quality of black state legislators appears to have been higher than their antebellum white counterparts.

The Reconstruction Act of 1867 divided the South into districts and placed it under military control. It also provided for constitutional conventions to set up new grounds for state governments. The new state constitutions allowed blacks to hold public office and as a result they served in practically all state government positions. Blacks served in all of the southern

98

state legislatures during Reconstruction. They served as lieutenant governor and secretary of state in South Carolina, Mississippi, and Louisiana. They also held some high state positions in Florida. P. B. S. Pinchback and Oscar James Dunn of Louisiana and John R. Lynch from Mississippi were prominent among these black leaders.

One indicator of achievement by the black lawmakers is that the state constitutions written by the so-called "Black Reconstruction" governments remained in force long after 1876 when blacks began to lose their legislative seats. The Reconstruction state legislatures provided for expanded suffrage for poor whites by removing all property qualifications for voting and holding office, they provided free public education for all, they exempted small property holders from taxation, they declared punishments such as whipping and branding to be illegal, and most importantly, they established an active state militia. Generally, the black legislators pressed for no special advantages for former slaves nor were they revengeful or vindictive. Mississippi's black lawmakers even petitioned Congress to remove all political disabilities from whites (Stampp, 1965).

The black lawmakers were mostly conservatives and all they asked for was equal political rights and equality before the law. They had no desire for political parties divided along racial lines, they made no attempt to transfer complete political control to blacks, and they were convinced that if the race issue was dropped they could function with whites within the existing party framework. They were particularly careful not to push for integrated schools because they recognized the overwhelming opposition whites held for that measure. Most of them were willing to postpone action on social segregation and to concentrate their efforts on civil and political rights. Despite this conservative stance, the black lawmakers were unduly criticized by white conservatives, North and South, who held them with the utmost contempt and described them as "baboons, monkeys, mules, ragamuffins and jailbirds" (Stampp, 1965).

The constructive work by the black lawmakers was marred by evidences of fraud and corruption in some states. But fraud and corruption were not new to the South nor to the nation. Moreover, extravagance and mismanagement flourished all over the nation in the years following the Civil War.

African American Congressmen were not destined to leave any mark on national legislation. During Reconstruction fourteen blacks from the South were elected to the United States House of Representatives. Six of them were from South Carolina. Only two blacks, Hiram R. Revels and Blanche K. Bruce from Mississippi, served in the United States Senate. The charge that black Congressmen were unprepared is fallacious. Some black leaders were brilliant. John Mercer Langston had been the Inspector-General of the Freedman's Bureau and in 1890 was seated as a representative from Virginia, Robert B. Elliott served two terms from South Carolina, and George Henry White, the last of the black Reconstruction legislators was a teacher from North Carolina. Furthermore, the records show that:

> "most of the major Negro leaders had more formal education than Abraham Lincoln. Ten of the 22 Negroes who served in Congress had attended College and five were lawyers. Both Negro Senators had attended college . . . and both were infinitely superior to . . . other men Mississippi would send to the Senate" (Bennett, 1962, p. 203).

Further complicating the efforts of the black lawmakers was the fact that they had little help from southern whites. The southern white population generally sided with the Democrats and they were not sympathetic to the black lawmakers despite the accrued benefits. Not corruption but honesty, not ignorance but competence horrified many southern whites who feared that if the new regimes which contained African American participation were successful a dangerous black precedent would be established. Moreover, the most capable white men in the South took no active interests in rebuilding the governments they had torn down, and they allowed them to be reconstructed "with untempered mortar" (Williams, 1883).

## The Black Vote

The election of 1868 clearly reflected the changes that had taken place in the South as Ulysses S. Grant swept the South by virtue of the black vote. During this election the black masses were stirred by an unparalleled ferment of political activity. African Americans flocked to huge open-air meetings, they heavily registered to vote, and they skillfully organized political groups. The white South was stunned by black demonstrations of political ingenuity in the lower political spectrum. The 1868 election fully revealed the importance of the black vote which overwhelmingly favored Grant. But without the 450,000 black votes cast for him, Grant would have been perilously close to defeat.

The black vote was the key and the foundation for the radical changes taking place in the South. Black preachers were noted as "the great power" in controlling and uniting black voters. But these changes in the South's political and social structure were not truly democratic because they were forced by the North at the point of the sword. The question was how long would the North, which at no time experienced such cataclysmic political and social changes, be content to support black enfranchisement. Moreover, how could the North remove the mote of racial injustice from the eye of the South when the North was partially blind itself?

Radical Republicans in the North who forced voting rights for southern blacks were embarrassed that blacks could not vote in most northern states. At the end of the Civil War several northern states had rejected proposals to allow blacks to vote. Only six states (Maine, New Hampshire, Vermont, Massachusetts, Rhode Island, and New York) allowed blacks to vote. Northern blacks launched a massive campaign to convert the remaining states but they were successful in adding only three (Iowa, Minnesota, and Wisconsin) to the fold.

The black vote was also important in the North where changes were not so radical but were capstoned in the Declaration of Independence. Black leaders such as Frederick Douglass, J. Sella Martin of New York, George T. Downing of Rhode Island, Peter H. Clark and John M. Langston of Ohio, and Martin R. Delaney and Robert Purvis of Pennsylvania formed the nucleus of a group which agitated for equal rights. They identified themselves with the patriots of 1776 who had fought for natural rights to life, liberty, and the pursuit of happiness. They were joined by black Civil War veterans and black newspaper editors.

Thaddeus Stevens, Pennsylvania Congressman called "the scourge of the South" because he vigorously championed black civil rights during Reconstruction. (Library of Congress photo.)

Politically, African Americans had no choice but to support the Republican Party. But it soon became evident that white Republicans were nearly as slothful as white Democrats when it pertained to the protection of black people's rights. Some African Americans like T. Thomas Fortune, editor of the *New York Age*, advocated bolting to a third party. Frederic Douglass discouraged such "political heresy" as wasting the black vote. Most African Americans in the North continued to support the Republican Party for many decades to come because it was the Party that had delivered the Emancipation Proclamation. P. B. S. Pinchback of Louisiana adequately described this dilemma by exclaiming that African Americans were caught "between the hawk of Republican demagogiasm and the buzzards of Democratic prejudice" (Lewis, 1965).

In the interim, African Americans were too politically unsophisticated to realize that the decisions affecting them were influenced by forces in the Second Industrial Revolution that began after the Civil War. Indeed, the Republican Party may have spawned the Emancipation Proclamation but it also capitulated for the sake of reconstructing the nation and facilitating northern industrialization.

## Reconstruction Education

Southern whites were more tolerant of educational institutions established for black improvement. African Americans seized this opportunity as a means to escape the increasing proscriptions and indignities that whites began to inflict upon them. The pursuit of education became an important part of black family life and great sacrifices and efforts were made for black children to go to school. Since public-supported schools were not in abundance for blacks, denominational boards in the major black churches provided funds for black education. In the meantime, the Freedmen's Bureau which had provided some education for African Americans was disbanded.

Concurrent with Reconstruction, a new group of wealthy white Americans emerged in the North to establish large foundations for black and white education. Among these were the George Peabody Education Fund established in 1867 to promote and encourage intellectual, moral, and industrial education among destitute southerners. The John F. Slater Fund was established in 1882 to uplift "the lately emancipated population of the Southern states and their posterity, by conferring upon them the blessings of Christian education" (Franklin, 1974). Black education benefitted from these foundations which increased in number in the next decades. However, when public funds for education became available, southern whites used the foundations to rationalize for the wide disparity in public support for segregated black and white schools. This disparity allowed white schools to receive funds that subsequently reached as high as five times that afforded black schools, and it persisted well past the mid-twentieth-century.

Segregated schools were a disservice to both African Americans and whites in the South as the inequities therein persisted and increased. White children, even those with less aptitude, were taught by the superior advantages they inherited that they were part of some master race. On the other hand, black children had to endure the badge of inferiority imposed upon them and at the same time keep faith in democracy. These conditions served to drive the races further apart. Moreover, educated African Americans began to see the humiliation of segregation and hesitated to intrude where they could suffer insult and more humiliation. The result was less sympathy between African Americans and whites than there was even during slavery. Segregated schools were accompanied by separate communities, separate churches, and separate public gatherings, all of which contributed to a basic distrust between the races. Franklin (1965) summarizes the destructive educational process that became entrenched during Reconstruction:

> "For both Negro and white children, one of the most effective lessons taught in Jim Crow schools was that even in institutions dedicated to training the mind a greater premium was placed on color than on brains. True education in the South was languishing. Only Jim Crow was flourishing and making steady gains in the generation after the Civil War" (p.148).

Despite these restrictions the greatest success among African Americans during Reconstruction was realized in education. In 1865 only three percent of African Americans were literate. In 1870 black literacy rose to 21 percent, and by 1895 it was up to 50 percent. It was during this period that black learning insti-

South Carolina Legislature around 1867, the first legislature in the state after the Civil War. (Library of Congress photo.)

tutions such as Howard University, Hampton Institute, Atlanta University, and Fisk University were founded. The founding of black schools of higher education was very important and they gave African Americans a sense of pride and dignity.

With the establishment of public schools for whites in the South after the Civil War, segregated schools for African Americans were also started. But in the North where public schools had been functioning since the antebellum years, the race policy varied. For example, New York City schools were completely segregated but Rochester, New York schools were integrated.

The Reconstruction effort, which included black participation and enfranchisement, may have been a failure as some historians claim. But it gave African Americans a taste of the elements that they would confront for the next century: civil rights, segregation, education, political and economic power, and racial unity. However, the overriding challenge that would persist and transcend all others would be white America's reluctance to accept black people as first-class citizens.

# CHAPTER X

## Black Leaders in Reconstruction

*'Tis a long way from slavery to freedom. Sometimes the freedman
is absolutely incapable of becoming a freeman.*
                                        *Charles V. Roman-1916*

The Reconstruction period following the Civil War was a
massive effort to bind the nation's wounds and re-unite the
Confederate states with the Union States. In that period black
people finally came to be viewed as individuals and their rights
as Americans citizens were a matter of open and great discussion. In fact, the discussion of these rights characterized the
Reconstruction period more than any other single issue.

During Reconstruction African Americans in the South were
elected to prominent federal and state positions at levels and in
numbers not known before or since. In the North they did not
have the votes to realize such political accomplishments but
some became prominent in education, the diplomatic services,
and entrepreneurship. However, during Reconstruction African
Americans were severely criticized and taunted by most whites
who did not want to compete with them on any level of equality.

# In the South

Hiram R. Revels was the first black man to serve in the United States Senate and was elected from Mississippi in 1870 to fill the seat formerly occupied by Jefferson Davis. He was a free black from North Carolina who had lived in Indiana, Ohio, and Illinois and was educated in a seminary in Ohio and at Knox College in Illinois. He was an ordained minister in the African Methodist Episcopal Church, he had taught school, and he founded a school for freedmen in St. Louis, Missouri. During the Civil War he was a recruiter and later served as an army chaplain for a Mississippi black regiment. He settled in Natchez, Mississippi after the War, became prominent in state politics, and worked diligently in the interest of his state. As a Senator he joined other black lawmakers in pushing for the removal of all disqualifications on ex-Confederates.

Blanche K. Bruce was the second black to serve in the United States Senate and he also was elected from Mississippi. A Virginia born slave, he escaped during the Civil War and established a school for blacks in Hannibal, Missouri. He studied at Oberlin College and migrated to Mississippi in 1869 to enter politics. He served as a tax collector, sheriff, and superintendent of schools in Floreyville before being elected to the Senate in 1874. He was noted as the "silent Senator," he was an active politician, but he never wielded great influence. His most notable service was with the Manufactures, Education, and Labor Committee and also the Pensions Committee.

P. B. S. Pinchback was one of three African Americans who served as Lieutenant Governor in Louisiana during Reconstruction and was one of the most important and controversial figures from that state. During the Civil War he served as a captain in the Union Army and was attached to General Benjamin Butler's *Corps d' Afrique* which was staffed entirely by black officers. After the War he became the editor and publisher of a weekly newspaper called the *New Orleans Louisianian*. He became Lieutenant Governor in 1871 when Oscar James Dunn, who was also black, died in office. In 1872 he was elected to Congress and also to the United States Senate but was denied his seat in both outcomes. For forty-three days in 1873 he was the acting governor of Louisiana. He used his

JOHN M. LANGSTON.

John Mercer Langston, notable black lawyer and politician who before
and after the Civil War fought for black civil rights. (Photo courtesy of
Atlanta University Center Archives.)

newspaper to criticize the Republican Party for failing to pass the Force bills, their omission of the school clause from the Civil Rights bill, and their refusal to seat black contestants in Congress. He was a strong supporter of universal suffrage, free public schools, and guaranteed civil rights for all people.

When John Mercer Langston was elected as clerk of the township in Brownhelm, Ohio in 1855 he became the first black man to be elected to public office in the United States. Born a Virginia slave and the son of a white plantation owner, he was educated by some white friends of his father. When his father died the friends took him to Ohio to study at Oberlin College. There he received bachelors and masters degrees and was admitted to the bar in 1854. In his law practice, he often defended abolitionists and was a leading spokesman against taxing African Americans without giving them the right to vote.

In 1859 Langston declined an offer made by John Brown to accompany him to Harpers Ferry, Virginia, but during the Civil War he was an effective recruiter for black troops. He founded and organized the Law Department at Howard University in 1869 and served as a dean, vice president, and acting president at Howard. He sat on the Board of Health during the Grant administration and was the Minister of Haiti under President Rutherford B. Hayes. In 1888 he was elected to the United States Congress as a representative from Virginia but was not seated until 1890. He was noted for advocating redress for wrongs committed against African Americans through the state and federal courts.

Henry M. Turner of the African Methodist Episcopal (AME) Church was the acknowledged spiritual leader of blacks in Georgia and a well-known political activist for civil rights. He was born of free parents in 1834 near Abbeville, South Carolina. After his father died he worked in the cotton fields with slaves, was apprenticed to a blacksmith, and learned to read at the age of fifteen with the aid of liberal whites. He joined the Methodist Episcopal Church in 1851, became an itinerant preacher, and switched to the AME Church in 1858. He pastored in Baltimore and Washington, D.C. and attracted the attention of President Abraham Lincoln who in 1863 made him a chaplain in the Union Army, the first black man to hold such a position.

During Reconstruction Turner was assigned by President Andrew Johnson to the Freedmens Bureau in Georgia, but he later resigned to build up the AME Church in that state. He was one of the founders of the Republican Party in Georgia. He was elected a delegate to the Constitutional Convention in 1867 and to the state legislature in 1868. He was known as the most anti-white and the most disliked of the black legislators, but he sponsored fair treatment for all Georgia citizens. He returned to the AME church in 1870 to hold several responsible positions and became a bishop in 1892. Turner became disillusioned with America in 1874 and was best known as the leading advocate for African colonization during the late nineteenth and early twentieth-centuries.

Black philanthropists also made their mark during Reconstruction. Thomy Lafon of New Orleans was a qualified teacher who became a merchant and real estate investor. He became one of the city's richest men and spent most of his life helping the needy regardless of their race, creed, or color. At one time the city borrowed money from him and upon his death he left $600,000 to charity. Wheeling Gaunt of Kentucky also made a fortune in real estate. He migrated to Ohio in the 1860s and left a substantial endowment for worthy students of Wilberforce University. Wheeling Gaunt Park in Yellow Springs, Ohio stands today as a tribute to Gaunt's concern for needy widows.

## In the North

In the North black intellectuals had some freedom of opportunity, notably in the field of education. William S. Scarborough became the first black scholar of note. Born in Georgia, he was gifted in languages to the extent of becoming an expert in Greek, Latin, Hebrew, Sanskrit, and the Slavic languages. In 1887 he became a professor of Greek at Wilberforce University and later was elected its president. Other black educators of note during Reconstruction included Richard T. Greener who helped develop the public school system of South Carolina and became the Dean of Howard University in 1879. William H. Crogman taught extensively in the South and became the first black President of Clark University in Atlanta. Also, Peter Humphries Clark, who as a young man was active in the Underground Railroad, later made substantial contributions to the public school system of Cincinnati, Ohio. It was men such as these who helped fill the educational gap created by generations of slave illiteracy.

The Reconstruction period ran concurrent with the Second Industrial Revolution which transformed American economic life and elevated the nation to worldwide industrial preeminence. Black participation in the Second Industrial Revolution was generally confined to menial tasks, but black inventors still made substantial contributions. For example, Granville T. Woods of Ohio opened a factory in Cincinnati for the manufacture of telephone, telegraph, and electrical equipment. He invented a steam boiler furnace in 1884, and later produced fifteen patented devices for electrical railways and a telegraphic device for transmitting messages between moving trains.

In other business-industry areas, Norbert Rilleux (noted in Chapter I) added to his contributions by designing a method for handling sewage which could have removed the menace of yellow fever from New Orleans, but it was never adopted. Jan Ernst Matzeliger was born in Dutch Guiana and earned passage to the United States as a sailor. He invented the lasting machine in 1883 which revolutionized the manufacture of shoes and helped to make Lynn, Massachusetts the shoe capitol of the world. Little publicity was given to these men as being black. Americans continued to build false stereotypes about black people despite these important contributions to technology, industry, and society.

Ebenezer D. Bassett became the first black diplomat abroad and was appointed by President Ulysses S. Grant as the minister resident to Haiti in 1869. He was so effective that upon completion of this assignment in 1877, the Haitian government appointed him to be their consul to the United States for ten years. Also serving in the diplomatic service at this time was John Henry Smythe. As a Wilmington, Delaware lawyer and politician, Smythe exerted great efforts in the controversial presidential election of 1876, and was later named as the United States minister to Liberia. Later in Liberia, he served as the representative of several European governments.

The most prominent black historian of this period was George Washington Williams. He enlisted in the Union Army at the age of 14 to fight for black freedom in the Civil War, and later served in the Mexican Army. He then reenlisted in the United States Army and served in the Tenth Cavalry to fight the Comanches. In 1868 he returned home to Massachusetts to complete studies at the Newton Theological Seminary and pastored in Boston for a few years. He then moved to Cincinnati, studied law, and was admitted to practice in the state of Ohio. In 1879 he was elected to the Ohio legislature. He wrote articles in the *Cincinnati Commercial* under the pen name of "Aristides." In 1883 after years of diligent research, he wrote his two-volume *History of the Negro Race in America From 1619 to 1880*. It later was considered to be the most definitive work on black history written in the nineteenth-century. He died on an extended visit to Africa at the age of forty-one.

W. E. B. DuBois was to make his biggest impact on black affairs in the twentieth-century; however, by 1895 he was emerging as a young black militant leader who was schooled at Fisk University and was the first black to receive a Ph.D. from Harvard University. A native of Massachusetts, he also studied in Germany. He would later take issue with Booker T. Washington's social philosophy, and was generally recognized as one of the most incisive thinkers and effective platform orators in the United States. He was also one of the most profound scholars of his generation.

George C. Hall, one of the founders of Provident Hospital in Chicago, was a physician who helped to further develop the skills of other black surgeons. By organizing clinical demonstrations in surgery, Dr. Hall developed a program of continuing education for black doctors that was used throughout the United States. He also helped to establish infirmaries in cities throughout the South.

Although African Americans served in the armed services with distinction in every American war, the first black to graduate from The United States Military Academy at West Point was Henry Ossian Flipper in 1877. Flipper was the son of a Georgia slave and endured hostility and inhuman treatment from white cadets and white instructors at West Point. Other black cadets had tried West Point, but even with support from the President

Henry Ossian Flipper, first black West Point graduate. (Photo courtesy of William L. Katz Collection.)

of the United States they were driven to resign. Upon his graduation, Flipper was assigned to the Tenth Cavalry, but in 1881 he was charged and tried for "embezzling public funds and conduct unbecoming an officer." He was found guilty on the second charge, was discharged, and spent several years thereafter trying to prove his innocence. He was subsequently assigned to one of two all black regular army units to become an outstanding petroleum engineer.

Only two other African Americans survived the racial hostility prevalent at West Point in the nineteenth century to graduate: John Alexander in 1887 who was assigned to the Ninth Cavalry, and Charles Young in 1889 who was assigned to the Tenth Cavalry. Thereafter, racism became so intense in the United States Army that the next black to graduate from West Point was nearly 50 years later in 1936.

African Americans in the nineteenth-century were even less successful in becoming academy graduate naval officers despite the fact that they had served in the United States Navy for decades. For example, in the War of 1812 blacks comprised 25 percent of the naval forces under Admiral Oliver Hazzard Perry when he defeated the British in the Battle of Lake Erie. Blacks participated in the Union Navy at that same level during the Civil War. In 1872 James Conyers of South Carolina became the first African American to be admitted as a midshipman to the United States Naval Academy at Annapolis, Maryland. But like most of his army counterparts, he was forced to resign the following year because of racial policies. Hence, Annapolis did not graduate its first black midshipman until seventy-six years later in 1949.

John P. Green was a black lawyer who gained prominent status in the North. After graduating from The Cleveland Law School in Cleveland, Ohio in 1870, he served three terms as Justice of the Peace in Cuyahoga County. In 1881 at the age of thirty-six, Green was elected to the Ohio State legislature and was noted for his clear impressive speaking. In 1892 he became the first black to be elected to the Ohio Senate. He was a close friend of John D. Rockefeller and other prominent Republican leaders at the national level. His political career reflected the fact that Ohio was the leader among all northern states in appointing and electing black men to responsible public positions during Reconstruction (Williams, 1883).

These were some of the prominent African Americans of Reconstruction who joined the ranks of Frederick Douglass and others. They patiently worked within the socio-political system to deliver a new order that would benefit all Americans. They faced overwhelming odds of racial proscriptions, but their faith in the United States Constitution buttressed their pursuits towards the American Dream. Also, they were convinced that black enfranchisement was the key for making that Dream a reality.

# CHAPTER XI

## The Thorns of Disenfranchisement

*Injustice anywhere*
*is a threat to justice everywhere.*
Martin Luther King, Jr.-1963

The new status afforded African Americans during Reconstruction did not meet with the approval of most southern whites. Black enfranchisement infuriated most whites and they were determined to do something about it. Local black leaders bore the brunt of the sustained assault by which whites undermined Reconstruction. By destroying the local black leaders, whites destroyed the black political foundation to leave the major leaders dangling in the air. One by one local black leaders were killed, driven out of the state, or compromised. In Mississippi, for example, a black state senator was killed in broad daylight.

Out of this racism and fear rose the Ku Klux Klan, one of the most inhuman and barbaric organizations. It originally began in 1865 in Tennessee and quickly spread throughout the South and parts of the North. Its mode of operation was brutal, violent, and vicious attacks on blacks and whites who

117

An August 3, 1872 *Harpers Weekly* presentation depicting the plight of the freedmen with a Republican on his right, a Democrat on his left, and two members of the Ku Klux Klan standing over the slain bodies of his family. The caption reads "It's Only a Truce To Regain Power." (Photo courtesy of Atlanta University Center Archives.)

befriended blacks. They cloaked their murderous deeds in the flowery rhetoric of the old South claiming that their only purpose was to maintain and protect southern honor, purity, and virtue. Lynchings, brutal murders, white hoods, and fiery crosses became their trademark as they executed their plan to reduce blacks to political impotence. The Ku Klux Klan was particularly attractive to poor southern whites who began to fear that African Americans might surpass them on the socioeconomic ladder. Since the Klan's main objective was "to protect white womanhood," there is strong evidence that their campaigns were largely directed against matings between black men and white women. However, they did not voice strong objections against out-of-wedlock matings between white men and black women.

## Southern Redemption

By 1874 only South Carolina, Florida, Louisiana, and Mississippi retained their Republican governments with black participation. Southern white Democrats identified themselves as the "Redeemers" of the South. They were up in arms and publicly exhorted their aims. In one white newspaper they exclaimed:

"We must render this a white man's government, or convert the land into a Negro man's cemetery" (Bennett, 1962, p. 213).

Open violence pervaded the South as moderate newspapers and periodicals were whipped into line by white Democrats to publicly defile all black politicians. General John McEnery, the Louisiana strongman exclaimed:

"We [the whites] shall carry the next election if we have to ride saddle-deep in blood to do it" (Bennett, 1962, p. 213).

The black population was systematically disarmed as the homes of African Americans were searched on any pretext. Ballot box manipulations reached amazing heights, polling places had armed guards of white men stationed nearby to keep blacks from voting, and the governors in each state disarmed or emasculated the black state militias. Such were the actions which blazed the path for southern redemption. Stampp (1965) adequately defines "southern redemption," a term coined by the Redeemers:

". . . meant that the federal government had renounced responsibility for reconstruction, abandoned the Negro, and, in effect, invited southern white men to formulate their own program of political, social, and economic readjustment" (pp. 186-187).

Economic pressure was also used by the Redeemers. Black Republicans could not find work, their wives could not buy supplies, and their children were refused medical attention. White Republicans were ostracized, their children hounded in school, and their wives snubbed in the churches. Whites were coerced to either leave the South or join the Democratic Party. In short, the Redeemers meant to use any means to pursue their end. The black Republicans fought back but their resources were meager since the Redeemers controlled the money, the land, and the credit facilities. African Americans were too unarmed and unorganized to meet such a formidable foe.

The convict-lease system facilitated southern redemption and it proved to be a scourge upon black men in the South. Established right after the Civil War when the southern states were unable to support appropriate penal institutions, the system allowed for convicted criminals to be hired out or leased to private interests. The private interests obtained a plentiful source of labor where they paid a small leasing fee to the state and the convicts received no pay for their services. Instead, the convicts (90 percent of whom were black men in most states) were subject to brutal treatment which was often fatal without redress. The brutality of the system reached staggering proportions and was comparable to the atrocities committed during the era of the Roman convict-slave galleys. Great fortunes were built under the convict-lease system as greedy entrepreneurs collaborated with corrupt state officials to exploit the South's labor pool. Also, the system served to deny employment to the free labor force in railroad construction and other projects badly needed for Reconstruction.

A principle factor in the victory of southern redemption was the North's loss of interest in continuing to punish the South. The term "punish" is appropriate because nowhere in the North did they implement black enfranchisement to the extent that they had forced it upon the South. By 1876 big business was firmly in the midst of the Second Industrial Revolution, and northern industrialists had begun to think seriously about southern markets and trade. The chaos and confusion that existed under southern Reconstruction was not conducive to northern business interests. The Compromise of 1877, therefore, was business-oriented and totally commensurate with northern racism and indifference.

The Compromise of 1877 allowed Rutherford B. Hayes to remove federal troops from the South in return for his receiving southern support in the election for President. The election was generated by a tie vote between Hayes and the Democrat candidate Samuel B. Tilden in 1876 and was set up by a specially created Electoral Commission. Thus, black voters had the rug pulled out from under them as federal troops in the South were withdrawn and the Redeemers ruthlessly took over. To stifle any twinges of conscience about forsaking African Americans, the national Republicans and President Hayes saw to it that lucrative federal appointed posts were given to top black leaders such as Frederick Douglass, John M. Langston, Blanche K. Bruce, and Robert Elliott.

With the white conservative victory the South confirmed the process of southern redemption and the whipping of African Americans into further submission. Men, North and South, immersed themselves in racial myths such as the black man being contented as a slave and wretched as a free man. Subsequently, the essential emphasis of the Civil War would be depleted and the bloody conflict would become an agency of reconciliation between the North and the South.

## The New Order

The Redeemers established a new order of social stratification in the South and the principal aim was that the "Negro dominance" of Reconstruction would never be repeated. Abandoned by the Union Army and their northern protectors and having little or no recourse from local laws, southern African Americans were forced into a new caste system that in some ways rivaled slavery. The new order was not based on law as was slavery, but on innate biological inferiority. African Americans, regardless of education, character, or personal merit, were cast at the bottom of the social ladder. Moreover, concerted efforts were developed to insure that they would not rise above that lowly position.

Even poor whites, who during slavery had to look up to some prominant blacks, were given an exalted status over all African Americans. Social segregation was the primary enforcer of the new order and racial intermarriage was deemed to be its greatest enemy. Extreme, tight segregation was seen as the best means to prevent miscegenation and the "mongrelization of the white race." The result was an economic peonage to which blacks found themselves tightly bound with no escape in sight.

The Redeemers surpassed their most ambitious expectations. The common white populace was continuously duped with lurid tales of Reconstruction, and the complicated voting systems designed to disenfranchise African Americans also led to a decline in the number of white voters. This significant withdrawal from the political life of the South facilitated "divide and rule" measures that were enjoined by the ruling planter class who wielded power highly disproportionate to their numbers.

The ignoble success of southern redemption was a retreat from democracy which deferred the American Dream, and for several decades it confounded black and white efforts to live peaceably as American citizens. In this milieu, the systems designed for black subordination were strengthened, agriculture in the South recovered as a way of life, and the planter class resumed its antebellum role of paternal despot. Franklin (1961) adequately describes this dilemma:

"In every important social relationship the Negro was kept at a "safe distance", . . . the Negro had to build institutions completely separate from those of the whites, . . . these institutions contributed to the emergence of a Negro world with all the trappings of an entirely separate community. Suspicion and distrust were the inevitable by-products of such racial division" (p. 224).

## Jim Crow Confirmed

Although a Republican dominated Congress passed a Civil Rights Act in 1875, the Redeemers were aided by the Supreme Court which consistently interpreted the Fourteenth and Fifteenth Amendments in such a way as to weaken the protection of African Americans. In 1883 the Supreme Court struck down the Civil Rights Act of 1875 which not only sought to secure equal rights for all citizens in hotels, theaters, and public amusement, but also allowed for black participation on juries. African Americans were up in arms, holding many meetings, and heaping ridicule and invective on the Supreme Court; however, the laws concerning the Civil Rights Act of 1875 were rarely implemented anyway. The lower courts had failed to give the Act constitutional sanction or so narrowly interpreted it as to defeat its purpose.

United States Attorneys purposefully avoided civil action on behalf of African Americans. Civil action was costly and the number of cases pursued were small. The Supreme Court Decision of 1883 thus reflected the prevailing opinion of the times. Most white people received it as a "matter of course" (Philadelphia Times, 1883). Some Republicans and abolitionists complained but their chief spokesmen, Charles Sumner and Thaddeus Stevens, were dead. In the South Republicans and Democrats hailed the Decision and began to institutionalize Jim Crow practices. African Americans were depressed but had no viable alternatives.

Subsequently, eighteen northern states individually passed state civil rights laws which had relatively more protection for African Americans than the Civil Rights Act of 1875; however, many of these state laws were a mockery and an insult to black people. For example, in Ohio racial discrimination in roller rinks resulted in cases where one black plaintiff was awarded one cent (Cleveland Gazette, Jan. 31, 1885). The other seventeen states had similar situations as local traditions prevailed and accorded African Americans a place of inferiority. Many northern whites began to accept blacks on public conveyances, but in recreational facilities they tenaciously held the color line.

Black suffrage received a brief boost by the Populist Movement which swept the country in the 1880s. Agrarian leaders sought black support in the South, holding that poor whites and poor African Americans wallowed in the same economical strait jacket. Where Populism was successful at the polls as in North Carolina, African Americans secured such offices as alderman, magistrate, deputy sheriff, and port collector. Reviving the cry of "Negro dominance," defeated or ambitious white politicians charged that the Populists were taking the South back to the days of the carpetbagger. Such charges spelled doom to the

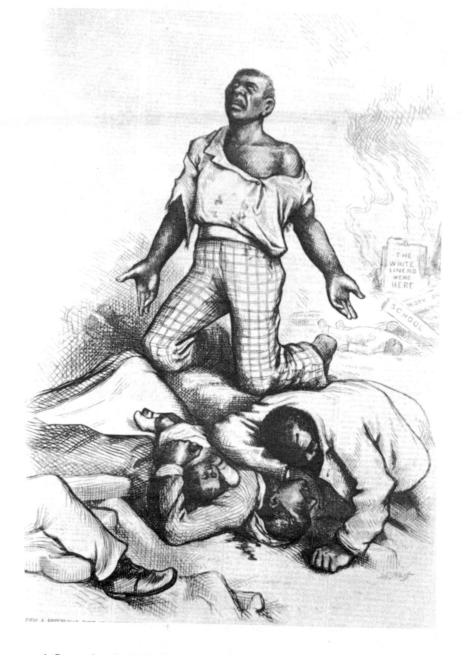

A September 2, 1876 *Harpers Weekly* presentation showing freedmen asking for equal protection under the laws. (Photo courtesy of Atlanta University Center Archives.)

new alliance of poor African Americans and poor whites, for in the South no political accusation was more fatal than that of being associated with black people. Although the Populist Movement was directly aimed to benefit poor white farmers, poor whites tended to forget everything whenever anyone shouted "Negro."

The Civil War and Reconstruction left southern whites the land, but they had no money or labor to develop it. Sharecropping was the answer to this problem. It bound African Americans to the land and also to the planter class almost as effectively as had slavery. African Americans were generally illiterate, and were usually cheated out of their share of the crop. This put them further in debt to the planters. Those who tried to leave the farms without paying their "debt" were usually fined and jailed. The fines were paid by sending the black tenant back to the same farm to work off the fine -- usually at less than a dollar a day. Because of the sharecropping system, race relations grew steadily worse as poor whites were pitted against African Americans in competition for jobs on the farms.

Near the end of the Reconstruction period, African Americans began to leave the South in large numbers. Most black migrants were penniless and destitute as was the case with the 60,000 who left for Kansas in 1879. The migrants made such an impact in Oklahoma that there was some talk about making the territory a black state. The exodus was not a political movement. It was a spontaneous act of desperation on the part of African Americans to escape the spirit of violence and persecution that existed in the South after the Compromise of 1877.

Much of this violence was committed against black women who continued to be sexually assaulted and harassed by undisciplined white men. In fact, African Americans who left the South commonly complained that the white men who inflicted the most violence against black men were often the same sexual offenders against black women. These conditions were reminiscent of those during plantation slavery when blacks had little or no protection from the law enforcement agencies. The result of the exodus was a redistribution of African Americans in areas of the North and the West which had been mostly white. This redistribution damaged the South's public image and discouraged northern whites from settling or investing in southern business enterprises.

By 1880 the thorns of disenfranchisement could be measured in terms of basic economics. The 1880 census showed that the economic status of southern African Americans had changed very little since the 1863 Emancipation Proclamation. Only a few of them had become landowners or businessmen and almost 90 percent worked for cash wages as farmers or servants. Less that 20 percent of the black farmers owned their own land, and in some districts the percentage was less than one percent. In Georgia where African Americans were nearly half the state population, they owned less than two percent of the land, only eight percent of the cattle and farm animals, and only five percent of the farm tools. It was truly stated that African Americans in that state "not only worked the white man's land but worked it with a white man's plow drawn by a white man's mule" (Clark and Kirwan, 1967).

C. Vann Woodward (1966) contends that southern whites during Reconstruction were given "a momentous assignment by history." They had an opportunity to abandon the racial assumptions of a lifetime and to uproot racial dogmas that were deeply imbedded in America culture. That momentous assignment was given to southern whites because, for good or ill, the South was America's theater and laboratory for improved racial relations. The legacy of slavery and the massive presence of African Americans in the South was a constant reminder of serious flaws and inconsistencies in the American creed. But it was an age of American imperialism which nationally carried direct implications of white supremacy. Consequently, southern whites rejected this momentous assignment, and the entire nation acquiesced in the South's racial policies of proscription.

The experiences of the white South during Reconstruction and southern redemption turned into a legend almost diametric with truth and fact. Aided by racist white historians, southern writers metamorphosed the southern planter class into aristocrats whose lineages could be traced to Anglo-Saxon kings. They glorified the Civil War as a lost cause which deserved a better fate, and Reconstruction became a wailing wall. As a result, the white South began to regard any undue interest by outsiders as "meddling," and a "leave us alone" psychology became greatly intensified.

Because of this mind-set, the white South's fetish for state sovereignty was revived and its hostility to outsiders became a phobia of immense proportions. African Americans increasingly became the targets of this phobia. As the nineteenth-century drew to a close, the future for black people was anything but bright. But as American citizens -- although consigned to a status of second-class -- they had an optimism that was tempered with courage. That courage would be sorely tested in the twentieth-century.

# CHAPTER XII

## The Folly of Appeasement

*The doctrine that submission to violence
is the best cure for violence did not hold good
as between slaves and overseers.
He was whipped oftener who was whipped easiest.*
                                        Frederick Douglass 1855

During the last two decades of the nineteenth-century, African Americans survived the period of southern redemption but most of the socioeconomic gains of Reconstruction were nullified. In the South southern redemption resulted in the return rule of the old antebellum white southern oligarchy coupled with strict Jim Crow laws to segregate the races and to keep African Americans in subservient roles. In the North it was concurrent with the economic boom of the Second Industrial Revolution which required more subtle forms of Jim Crow laws.

The Jim Crow laws reflected a milieu where there was virtually no vector of moral or spiritual conscience that could deter blatant white oppression. Many black leaders felt that concessions and acts of appeasement could mitigate the oppression.

Others were convinced that the only way to escape white oppression was to leave the South. African Americans viewed this dilemma as a lack of protection from the proper authorities; whites identified it as "the Negro problem" in America.

## Appeals to Leave the South

African Americans in the 1890s began to focus on Georgia, where the number of lynchings were the highest in the nation and where racial proscriptions were heavily protested. With little redress to their grievances, some frustrated black leaders became convinced that their strivings for first-class citizenship were futile, and they proposed three avenues of escape which caught the attention of many southern African Americans: a "Back-to-Africa" movement, exodus to the North, and colonization in the western frontier (Bacote, 1965).

The "Back-to-Africa" movement was strongly advocated by Bishop Henry M. Turner who had patiently tried to work with whites to provide civil rights and protection for African Americans in Georgia. He and others made sustained but abortive attempts to secure appropriations from Congress in support of voluntary colonization of African Americans in Africa, notably in Liberia. The "Back-to-Africa" movement reached its peak in 1892 when the Georgia legislature passed a new Jim Crow law, but few blacks actually chose to emigrate to Africa because most black leaders opposed the idea. Furthermore, testimony from African Americans who actually went to Africa and returned home was not favorable, and the returnees publicly denounced the movement and all those who sponsored it.

Black colonization to Africa and other areas outside the United States became a recurring theme that was alternately proposed by whites and African Americans well into the mid-1900s. Many whites proposed black colonization in the decades when it became apparent that black assimilation was a precursor for equal treatment under the law. Many African Americans proposed it in the decades of frustration when it became apparent that equal treatment under the law was virtually impossible. As far back as the early 1800s, blacks argued that their roots in Africa had been severed by the exigencies of slavery and that their heritage in America was as significant as any other ethnic group. Moreover, African Americans complained that colonization back to "the mother country" was never an issue when other ethnic groups were confronted.

A mass exodus to the North was suggested by some African Americans as the salvation of the race. They reasoned that the North was responsible for black emancipation and that northern teachers came South after the Civil War to preach social equality and to urge the protection of civil and political rights. It was thus postulated that by migrating to the North African Americans could realize the privileges that were associated with first-class citizenship. However, in the 1880s and the 1890s African Americans who left the South found conditions in the North anything but favorable. Although segregation was not as blatant as in the South, African Americans often found it difficult to find employment and many of the northern trade unions excluded them from membership.

Great pains were taken to prevent African Americans from competing with whites for available jobs in the North. Even highly qualified blacks were denied employment because some white workers threatened to strike if blacks were hired. In Boston and Chicago there were signs posted which read "No Negro help wanted." When white workers in Indiana learned that some African Americans were emigrating to that state to find work, they met them at the state line with guns and forced them back. Even the most educated blacks in the North had to settle for jobs as waiters, caterers, porters, or bartenders.

By 1895 the impact of Italian immigrants in many northern cities limited black job opportunities even further. The situation became so desperate that the responsibility for supporting the black family fell upon the women who were forced to take in washing or be hired out as domestics. Because of these limitations, a massive black exodus to the North did not become a viable option until World War I when job opportunities for African Americans became more plentiful.

Colonization to the western frontier was steeped in the premise that the federal government should set aside out of the public domain a separate state where African Americans could enjoy first-class citizenship. It was proposed by Bishop Lucius H. Holsey, a distinguished Georgian of the Colored Methodist Episcopal Church. He reasoned that the South's reluctance to

Booker T. Washington, educator and fund-raiser for black education, essayed a program of temporary social and political submission. (Photo courtesy of Atlanta University Center Archives.)

grant equal treatment to African Americans was not a southern problem, it was national in scope and involved national honor and federal law. On these grounds he requested that the federal government establish a black state in part of the Indian territory where whites would be ineligible for citizenship except through marriage, and the only whites who would be allowed to live there would be those with official connection with the government. But the federal government never took black colonization of the western frontier into serious consideration and most southern African Americans were not enthusiastic about such a separation.

The leaders of these movements brought some attention to the plight of African Americans, but they failed to convince southern blacks that their conditions would be improved by leaving the South. The black masses resigned to stay in the South with hopes that equal treatment would eventually prevail. Black leaders such as the Reverend Charles T. Walker, pastor of the Tabernacle Baptist Church in Augusta, Georgia, encouraged African Americans to stay in the South. He reasoned that prejudice was prevalent all over and inescapable in America. He argued that the North had fewer Jim Crow laws but the North did not offer the same economic securities as did the South. He also reasoned that it was only a matter of time when the most responsible whites in the South would come to aid and defend black rights. Some southern whites voiced agreement with Reverend Walker but offered no tangible solutions to the wave of white supremacy which grew in volume and intensity during the last decade of the nineteenth century (Vann Woodward, 1974).

## The Panacea of Education

These conditions set the stage for the emergence of Booker T. Washington, an outstanding black educator who promoted appeasement to white aggression. He was convinced that a policy of appeasement to white aggression was the only way that African Americans could enter America's socioeconomic mainstream.

Washington was educated at Hampton Institute in Virginia, and after a tenure of teaching there he was challenged to establish a similar school in Tuskeegee, Alabama. He built Tuskeegee Institute from the ground up and he was a dedicated educator who was praised by whites for his "soundness" on racial matters and his innovations in industrial education (identified as vocational education in modern times). In his school Washington taught young black women how to become proficient at cooking, sewing, and nursing. Young black men were taught the trades of carpenters, blacksmiths, plumbers, and painters. Although many African Americans of this period resented industrial education by connecting it with slavery, Washington's type of education developed character as well as vocational skills. He was America's leading proponent of education at a time when black schools and colleges depended heavily upon the philanthropic gestures of the white affluent.

White donors were convinced that Washington's emphasis on education was highly suitable for their interests, it would keep African Americans in the domestic services, and perpetually consign them to a status of inferiority. They therefore sought his assurance that their contributions would be earmarked for Washington's kind of education. Struggling black colleges subsequently added trades to their curriculum in order to obtain badly needed funds. By 1895 Washington, who was one of the most persuasive orators of his time, had gained a reputation as a great collector of funds for black education. It was at this point that he would put his stamp on so many aspects of African American life that its impact would be felt for the next sixty years. These conditions were typified by remarks once made by W. E. B. DuBois:

> "Not only did presidents of the U.S. consult Booker T. Washington, but governors and congressmen: philanthropists conferred with him, scholars wrote to him.... After a time almost no Negro institution could collect funds without the recommendation or acquiescence of Mr. Washington. Few political appointments (for blacks) were made anywhere in the U.S. without his consent....and his opposition was fatal" (Osofsky, 1967, p. 210).

Although Washington was not an elected leader, he represented a segment of African Americans who felt that no amount of black aggressiveness would meet with white approval in the 1890s. He essayed a program of appeasement, conciliation, and racial submission, and he refused to attack Jim Crow directly.

134

William E. B. DuBois, the reknown scholar who challenged Booker T.
Washington and demanded the social, economic, educational, and polit-
ical rights of full citizenship. (Photo courtesy of Atlanta University
Center Archives.)

Moreover, he urged African Americans to subordinate their political, social, and civil strivings for economic advancement. Washington refused to recognize that these factors must be linked together and that they cannot be pursued individually.

The depression-ridden 1890s were terrible times for African Americans who were experiencing a new surge of violence as well as economic repression from whites. In some liberal circles, whites felt guilty because of the national mood against African Americans and vainly searched for a solution to "the Negro problem." Among the solutions proposed was the revival of a plan by white racists for colonization back to Africa. The plan was proposed for all African Americans as an alternative to total assimilation. In the midst of these problems, Washington gained national recognition with a program and metaphoric statements that bailed out the conscience of white America and made him the most powerful man in the South as well as the most powerful black man in the nation.

Washington was asked to speak at the Atlanta Exposition on September 18, 1895. It was there that he voiced among a predominantly white crowd of high officials and dignitaries his social philosophy:

"In all things that are purely social we can be as separate as the fingers, yet one as the hand in all things essential to mutual progress" (Osofsky, 1967, p. 210).

Washington further stated that African Americans should forget about voting and public accommodations, and concentrate on making money. He reasoned that black agitation for social equality was unwise and that blacks should pull themselves up by their own bootstraps. The speech, later called the "Atlanta Compromise," made Washington famous in white circles. It was just what most white Americans wanted to hear from a black leader in order to salve the pains of conscience for the prevailing anti-black mood and the Supreme Court's recent Jim Crow decisions. From then on Washington received substantial contributions in funds earmarked for black education. Many white philanthropists and agencies felt that he had solved for all time "the Negro problem" in America.

Not all black leaders were convinced that Washington's social submission and industrial education were the panacea for the nation's racial proscriptions. W. E. B. DuBois and William Monroe Trotter steadfastly challenged Washington's policy and leadership, but they were subdued by the money and prestige that whites lavished on him in the name of education and progress. Even the most avid racists, such as Thomas Dixon Jr., a white Baptist minister who preached black inferiority, applauded Washington's speech. In short, Washington was just the tool needed by white America to whip African Americans into further submission.

## The Black Nadir

The violence that followed was unprecedented. Economic discrimination continued. Lynchings and murders reached staggering heights as many whites, feeling a new sense of race pride because of Washington's appeasement statement, virtually declared open season on all African Americans. Caste lines hardened and separate became more separate and less equal. Vann Woodward describes these conditions succinctly:

> "Washington's submissive philosophy must have appeared to some whites an invitation to further aggression . . . in proposing virtual retirement of the mass of Negroes from the political life of the South and in stressing a menial role that the race [blacks] was to play, he would seem unwittingly to have smoothed the path to proscription" (Vann Woodward, 1966, p. 82).

The 1890s has adequately been described as the nadir of black people's status in America. A black person was lynched on the average of one every two days. Lynchings were so common that white newspapers advertised them in advance and crowds came from afar on chartered trains to see them. White crowds devised more tantalizing tortures as black victims were roasted alive over slow fires. Sometimes the victims were women, white as well as black. Only a small percentage of the black victims were accused of rape. Most were charged with testifying against whites in court, seeking another job, using offensive language, failing to say "Mister" to a white man, attempting to vote, and being too prosperous. As Booker T. Washington "reigned" in Tuskeegee for the next twenty years following his speech of 1895, African Americans were the vic-

A lynch mob in 1893 gathers in an almost festive mood to watch the lynching of a black man accused of the murder of a three-year-old white girl. (Library of Congress photo.)

tims of more violence and aggression than at any time during their stay on the American continent (Logan, 1965).

Even Washington's educational program, though well intended, was a failure. The trades and crafts taught at Tuskeege Institute in the nineteenth-century were largely dependent upon philanthropic funds which did not keep pace with the technology of the Second Industrial Revolution. Washington's donors provided funding which was sufficient for training only in the obsolete trades and in the least desirable, least competitive jobs such as lumber mills, coal mining, railroad maintenance, and unskilled areas of manufacturing. The black graduates were excluded from the better paying jobs in the rising industrial economy, and in the towns and cities they were not employed in the prestigious occupations. They were generally confined to menial jobs such as delivery men, porters, janitors, and charwomen (Clark and Kirwan, 1967).

The educational curriculum deemed appropriate for African Americans in the 1890s had too much emphasis on industrial education. Industrial education consigned them to the domestic occupations, it tended to prepare them for what became known as "Negro jobs," and subsequently it became a vehicle for social control. In short, industrial education as prescribed for African Americans did not articulate with the Second Industrial Revolution and it did not prepare them to become viable in the workplace. Consequently, Washington's educational program was not replicated outside of Tuskeegee Institute.

Washington's lifestyle did not reflect his policy of appeasement. He publicly told African Americans that Jim Crow was irrelevant, but he violated the law by riding first-class in Pullman cars with southern white men and women. He advised them to forget about politics, while at the same time he wielded more political power than any black man in American history. However, few of Washington's white contemporaries knew of his private, unpublicized efforts to undermine segregation in public accommodations. He also covertly fought to eliminate discrimination against African Americans as jurors in court cases. Toward the end of his life in 1915, Washington began to see the folly of appeasement while moving closer to the position of his black opponents. But the die was cast in the 1895

Atlanta Compromise, and African Americans would have to face the socioeconomic repercussions for decades thereafter.

The folly of appeasement -- that total submission to aggression merely invites further aggression -- was not recognized by most African Americans during the 1840-1896 period. Most African Americans tenaciously held to the tenets of the American Dream, and they rationalized that since it became a reality for other ethnic groups, in time it would become a reality for them also. Unlike Irish Americans who in the 1840s engaged in bloody riots in the streets and Italian Americans who in the 1890s established powerful political machines, African Americans in the late nineteenth-century put their faith in the United States Constitution and were convinced that it subsequently would come to their aid and defense.

# CHAPTER XIII

## The Plessy v. Ferguson Decision

*It is human instinct to heed the cry of the oppressed.*
*But if the oppressed fail to give the outcry,*
*there will be no indication for the oppressor to heed.*
*Kelly Miller-1923*

In 1896 the United States Supreme Court Decision against Homer Plessy, a Louisiana male whose parentage was seven-eights white and one-eighth black, wrote into United States law the doctrine of racial separation and classification. In effect, the Supreme Court said that state laws requiring separate but equal accommodations for African Americans were a "reasonable use of state police power." Subsequently, it became the benchmark which supported state laws that segregated the races.

Plessy's main argument in his objection to being segregated on trains within the state of Louisiana was that if physical distinction such as color of skin could be used as a basis of segregation, then discrimination against blondes and redheads could also be considered reasonable and legal. Furthermore, Plessy argued that this segregation implied that African Americans

141

were inferior. Ironically, the Supreme Court in disputing Plessy's claims cited as precedent an earlier Decision passed in 1849 (Roberts v. City of Boston) which had been circumvented by the Massachusetts legislature.

## Southern Reactions

The Plessy v. Ferguson Decision encouraged whites in the South to launch another offensive to relegate African Americans to an inferior status, and on this front the Supreme Court would be firmly behind them. They legally stripped African Americans from voting by using the poll tax, grandfather clauses, residence requirements, and the ability to read or to interpret the state constitution. In many states tricky registration procedures were legalized to give local registrars broad powers to thwart black registration.

In 1890 Congress tried to pass a "Force Bill" which would have enforced the section of the Fourteenth Amendment concerning voting rights. Although it failed to pass, the South was more angered than alarmed. It aroused the South's spirit of defiance and thus fanned the zeal for further black disenfranchisement.

More than any other factor, the threat of a possible union between African Americans and the Populist Movement spurred southern whites to totally separate them from the ballot box. An indication of how successful whites were in just one state is reflected in the registration of black voters in Louisiana. Before the Plessy v. Ferguson Decision there were 130,344 black voters in Louisiana; in four years the number was reduced to 5,320 (Bennett, 1962).

The pattern was the same all over the South even in the South Carolina Sea Islands where the Port Royal Experiment had set the stage for amiable race relations in 1861. Ben Tillman, the South Carolina demagogue, publicly boasted:

"We have done our level best; we have scratched our heads to find out how we could eliminate the last one of them. We stuffed ballot boxes. We shot them [Negroes]. We are not ashamed of it" (Bennett, 1962, p. 235).

White politicians vividly kept alive the premise that black suffrage was a menace of all menaces. There was no surer way

142

of appealing to the white voter than by posing as a guardian of white suffrage, and candidates for public office vowed to outdo their opponents in keeping African Americans "in their place."

The Plessy v. Ferguson Decision led to additional aggression in other areas in the South. Before the Decision only three states had required Jim Crow waiting rooms. But after 1896 the other southern states developed similar Jim Crow laws. Coupled with the Atlanta Compromise the year before, the Plessy v. Ferguson Decision in the immediate years to follow would be the foundation for several Jim Crow laws. These laws would forcibly separate African Americans from whites in public transportation, sports, hospitals, orphanages, prisons, asylums, funeral homes, morgues, and cemeteries. Mobile, Alabama passed a 10 P.M. black curfew and Birmingham even passed laws to prevent African Americans and whites from playing checkers together.

African Americans were powerless to affect any constructive reaction to the Plessy v. Ferguson Decision. Black leaders organized, wrote resolutions, issued vague threats, and grasped at straws; all to no avail. If any black in the South had enough courage to complain to the local courts for redress of any wrong doing, he stood the chance of finding the onus somehow shifted to himself with results of him being sent away to the county chain gang.

The chain gangs were often used as schools for undisciplined young blacks in the period of southern redemption. They were real horror houses which had no parallel except in the persecutions of the Middle Ages and the concentration camps of twentieth-century Nazi Germany. Upon the slightest pretext young blacks were arrested, convicted, and leased to private individuals and companies who operated the chain gangs under the most inhuman conditions. The emasculating conditions to which black men were reduced in this era of hate and violence are graphically described by Bennett:

"Pinned against the wall by lynchings, proscription and organized programs, with every man's hand raised against them, Negroes flopped aimlessly, like a fish caught in the net. Intolerably oppressed by conditions which they did not understand and which they could not control, they moved from here to there . . . from one miserable hut to another ten miles down the road" (Bennett, 1962, p. 236).

## Northern Reactions

Northern reactions to the Plessy v. Ferguson Decision initially were more subdued. This was primarily due to the smaller percentage of African Americans in the North and the lesser apprehensions white northerners held for them in their presence. Although the North was never far apart from the South on racial policy, white northerners did not have the paranoia or "Negrophobia" that was prevalent in the South. But the North never experienced a slave society, the ravages of the Civil War, the humiliation of defeat, and the agony of Reconstruction. Hence, the lack of violent reactions to the Plessy v. Ferguson Decision in the North was not a reflection of northern liberalism or benevolence. As the black population increased in the North in the early 1900s, northern states and principalities joined the "Negrophobia" and copied the southern Jim Crow laws. Northern Jim Crow laws would in some cases become more devious and formidable than those in the South, and were subsequently characterized as "de facto segregation."

The Plessy v. Ferguson Decision put a legal stamp on American racism and consolidated the Atlanta Compromise. The two acts were separate and just months apart, but they affirmed that the American Dream would be deferred, and set the stage for decades of deprivation on yet another level. The time was ripe for such a subjugation of African Americans as the United States was emerging as the world's leading industrial power, and many whites were thoroughly convinced of their superiority among the races of mankind.

Although not apparent until decades later, the Plessy v. Ferguson Decision was a major setback in black-white relations in the United States. It is ironic that this setback occurred at a time in American history when the Progressive Movement was in its embryonic stages. One of the main issues of this Movement was social justice. After 1896 many social reforms were enacted for white Americans; however, as social justice improved for white Americans during the Progressive Movement, it concurrently declined for African Americans. Frederick Douglass lamented shortly before his death in 1895:

144

"It sometimes seems we are deserted by heaven and earth....If the American conscience were only half alive, if the American church and clergy were only half Christianized, if American moral sensibility were not hardened by persistent infliction of outrage and crime against colored people, a scream of horror, shame, and indignation would rise to Heaven..." (Ososfky, 1967, p. 165).

# CHAPTER XIV

## Reshuffling Black History

*The greatest and most immediate danger
of white culture, . . . is its fear of the Truth,
its childish belief in the efficacy of lies
as a method of human uplift."*
W. E. B. DuBois-1940

There is great precedent for historians to omit and distort facts -- economic, cultural, social, and military -- which are not popular or flattering to the contemporary scene. American historians of the late nineteenth-century and early twentieth-century would do no less concerning African Americans. They refused to accept black history at its face value, and rewrote or ignored it to suit the preconceptions and strutting ego of white America. In so doing, they violated every methodological tenet of the historian. Historical truths about African Americans have been so warped and omitted that it is no less than phenomenal. Moreover, that such a farce could be successful and perpetuated in a society that boasts its enlightenment is no less than amazing.

The late nineteenth-century American historians did not set this precedent. For more than 300 years in America the history of African Americans was ignored to such an extent that white Americans led themselves to believe that blacks had no history. There were no chairs for professors of African American history in the nation's colleges and universities. There were only a few black and white scholars digging into the dusty records of black people whose works were almost universally considered to be insignificant and inferior. In the late nineteenth-century, the efforts of these scholars were ignored when the assimilation of events concerning all Americans was considered. Most American historians then proceeded to write what white America wanted to read about black people, oftentimes completely ignoring documented facts concerning African Americans and whites interacting with each other. The end result was that future generations of African Americans would suffer an identity homicide, and the mis-education of all Americans would facilitate and augment racial polarization.

Many American historians of the twentieth-century would follow the lead of the Phillips-Burgess-Dunning school. This school of historical interpretation, consisting of prominent historians Ulrich B. Phillips, John William Burgess, and William A. Dunning, led early twentieth-century Americans to believe that African Americans were inherently happy, docile, and inferior creatures. The Phillips-Burgess-Dunning School did not reveal the facts relating to black revolts during slavery. Freedom fighters such as Gabriel Prosser, Denmark Vesey, and Nat Turner were labeled "insurrectionists" who did not represent a cross section of African Americans. But a closer look at history discloses that African Americans resisted slavery in every way imaginable, some to the point of committing suicide and even infanticide.

American historians in this period distorted black accomplishments in nearly every field, and presented slave holders such as Jefferson Davis, demagogues such as John C. Calhoun, and traitors such as Robert E. Lee as great and honorable men. Even American-made movies depicting the era of Civil War and Reconstruction deliberately wrote distortions or omitted facts in their scripts that denied black contributions and achievements. American movies have served as an important instru-

148

ment for learning, especially among the masses who have not seriously studied American history. But until recent decades, the Hollywood movie-makers drew few distinctions between fact and fiction when it concerned African Americans. Thus, the pernicious lies perpetrated about African Americans have no parallel in modern history.

This parody was destined to become successful because of the volatile events of the nineteenth-century. Moreover, the stereotypes resulting from the Atlanta Compromise and the Plessy v. Ferguson Decision virtually rendered it a certainty. Through the turn of the century, historians of the Phillips-Burgess-Dunning school began the systematic denigration of virile black performances in the Civil War. By 1928 W. E. Woodward, a biographer of Ulysses S. Grant, fallaciously wrote:

"the American negroes are the only people in the history of the world, so far as I know, that ever became free without any effort of their own. The Civil War was not their business. They had not started the war nor ended it. They twanged banjos around the railroad stations, sang melodious spirituals, and believed that some Yankee would soon come along and give each of them forty acres of land and a mule" (Woodward, 1928).

The essence of these words set the tenor of the times for decades in the twentieth-century. However, the truth is documented that Grant and even Abraham Lincoln expressed the opinion that black servicemen, who represented 10 percent of the Union Army and 25 percent of the Union Navy, helped turn the tide of the Civil War in favor of the Union. Moreover, the records show that African Americans played a vital role in Reconstruction and in the re-union of the United States.

With the relegation of African American history into obscurity and with the distortion and omission of pertinent facts, American historians reflected the ultra-racism of the late nineteenth-century. They set the pace for historians writing textbooks decades thereafter, and reinforced negative stereotypes and beliefs about African Americans. The belief that was bred in the nineteenth-century concerning the natural inferiority of African Americans is poignantly described by Katz (1987):

". . . this belief soon affected more than slave-ship captains, plantation masters and overseers. As bondage became entrenched, it became the *sine qua non* of southern life, taught to eight million whites from pulpit, schoolroom, newspapers, books, lecture halls and legal codes. Its argument drew from a spurious science, a twisted history and selected quotations from the Bible. Above all, it granted to each white a superior status over every black. Its impact on all whites was thus assured" (p. 305).

American revisionist historians since the 1960s have done much to correct unsubstantiated beliefs about African Americans, and they have brought a modicum of reason into the study of American history. No longer do pernicious lies and misconceptions go unchallenged in the textbooks of American schools and colleges, and the tenet that a lie cannot live forever is generally accepted. But the American Dream remains deferred, and the gauntlet is laid down for yet another generation -- perhaps in additional media -- to rekindle its vital messages.

# Epilogue

During the 100 years following the 1896 United States Supreme Court Plessy v. Ferguson Decision, black America witnessed substantial turmoil in its quest for social and economic advancement. In the first half of that century, the "separate but equal" tenet of the Plessy v. Ferguson Decision served to reduce African Americans to a low-caste level of existence. However, in the second half of that century, powerful sources were synthesized to move them toward assimilation in American culture and society.

At the turn of the century, the United States was emerging as a world industrial power with a strong emphasis on manufacturing. This spurred a mass black migration to the northern cities where there was hope for gainful employment, economic security, and less white oppression. African Americans were anxious to escape a new wave of white violence which resulted in major race riots in the South. Riots occurred in Greenwood, South Carolina and Wilmington, North Carolina in 1898 as well as in Atlanta, Georgia, and Brownsville, Texas in 1906. At the same time African Americans found little relief from violence in the North as a number of towns in Ohio and Indiana barred them from residence. Moreover, there were riots in northern cities such as Springfield, Ohio in 1904 and Springfield, Illinois in 1908.

In the early 1900s the National Association for the Advancement of Colored People (NAACP) began to be an option for dealing with forced social and economic subjugation. The NAACP was established in 1909 by W.E.B. DuBois, a group of his African American supporters, and white progressives sympathetic to equal rights. It was denounced by most whites, and some African Americans including Booker T. Washington, considered that the better survival tactic was accommodationism. The principal weapon of the NAACP was lawsuits in the federal courts which in their first decade produced some important legal victories. Although it was not a radical organization, in the early 1900s the NAACP stressed the opportunity for exceptional African Americans to gain full equality. The NAACP therefore did not initially secure the following of the black masses and was perceived as a force for the black bourgeoisie.

Decades later, however, it would change that image to emerge as the nation's leading organization for civil liberties.

When World War I increased the need for more workers in manufacturing, nearly a half million African Americans left the South and they were facilitated by northern labor agents who provided free transportation. This "Great Migration" started in 1915 resulted in a demographic shift in the African American population which was highly resented by northern white workers. Their resentment was based upon the premise that African Americans had lower wage demands than white workers. Consequently, a rash of race riots occurred in cities such as Philadelphia, Chicago, and East St. Louis resulting in a sharp increase in the number of lynchings. Within three months 120 people died in race riots in the "red summer" of 1919. African American factory workers faced an additional crisis when returning white veterans displaced them from their jobs, thereby creating widespread layoffs and unemployment in the black community.

World War I encouraged black enlistments in the military which resulted in 400,000 African Americans serving in the United States Army. Half of them served in Europe where they obtained a perspective on race relations they had not experienced before. They were placed in segregated command units under white officers who often held them in contempt; however, white Europeans gave them a respect and equal treatment they had not witnessed anywhere in the United States. They were convinced that upon their return home a nation grateful for their military services would correct the inequities of the past and provide the social justice that was being preached and advocated by white Americans. However, they were sorely disappointed. African Americans in the postwar years of World War I continued to suffer greatly from an inflamed climate of racism throughout the nation. In addition, African American veterans were cruelly disillusioned to find that the war that was fought and won in Europe to "save democracy" granted them no significant social or economic gains in the United States. Some black veterans were lynched while still wearing their uniform. The Ku Klux Klan reorganized in 1919 to become an even more effective terrorist group. They became so powerful that by

1926 they were marching openly and defiantly down the streets of major cities, including Washington, D.C.

The chaos and desperation that African Americans experienced during and after World War I set the stage for the revival of black colonization to Africa. Colonization to Africa in the early 1900s was led by Marcus Garvey, a Jamaican who arrived in the United States in 1916 to establish the Universal Negro Improvement Association. By 1919 he had established 30 branches and claimed a black membership of 4-6 million. Garvey appealed to race pride at a time when African Americans felt they had little to be proud of because their accomplishments were not widely disseminated. In his newspaper, the *Negro World*, he exalted everything black and insisted that black culture was superior to white culture. He proclaimed that it was futile to seek equal treatment from white Americans. Also, he encouraged African Americans to return to Africa where they could be better accepted. He was very popular among African Americans of darker complexion and they contributed hard earned monies to his 1921 plan to transport thousands to Africa aboard his Black Star Company of four steamships. The plan was aborted when the charismatic Garvey was jailed on questionable mail fraud charges in 1923 and deported as an undesirable alien in 1927.

Garvey's movement of pan-African nationalism was a reflection of black desperation and protest against the white racism of the postwar period. The movement was not supported by the NAACP and several of its prominent members contributed to Garvey's downfall. Garvey was especially contemptuous of W.E.B. DuBois while at the same time he showed disdain for most light-skinned African Americans. Nevertheless, the Universal Negro Improvement Association was the first mass movement among African Americans, and many of its race pride philosophies were carried forth to the second half of the twentieth-century.

African Americans made only limited gains in civil liberties before the beginning of World War II. When the stock market crashed in 1929, African Americans were already suffering from economic depression. As the Great Depression of the 1930s set in, their conditions worsened to the extent that 33 percent of African Americans who were employable required public assistance in 1935. For example, in Norfolk, Virginia 80 percent and in Atlanta, Georgia 65 percent of the black workforce were on public assistance. In the large cities African American men, women, and children roamed the streets searching garbage cans for food, often foraging with dogs and cats. Hence, World War II not only brought the United States out of the Great Depression, the job opportunities it helped to produce saved many blacks from outright starvation.

Many economically frustrated African Americans in the 1930s and 1940s deserted their churches to follow charismatic black religious leaders such as Father Divine and Daddy Grace who promised speedy transformations into a heaven on earth. Father Divine, born George Baker in 1864, developed a following based in Detroit, Michigan that was a social movement as well as a religious movement. He promoted himself as God and began preaching against racism, hunger, and segregation. His following, which included some white Americans, were housed in 75 missions which he called "heavens." In the 1930s they were firmly established in many eastern cities and Midwestern communities. Daddy Grace, born Charles M. Grace in 1882, had a similar following based in Washington, D.C., and he too made a claim to be God. He preached against fornication, lying, and stealing, and his services were noted for their erotic singing and dancing with great frenzy. He established 67 Houses of Prayer primarily in northeastern cities and a few in the southeast. Father Divine and Daddy Grace were two of the most colorful religious figures to mount a pulpit in American history, and they capitalized on the meager participation that African Americans had in this society. They became multi-millionaires (one member left Father Divine a 10 million-dollar estate) with world-wide memberships primarily with the support of African Americans who immigrated to northern cities. Their following reflected African Americans' intense desire to move closer to some supernatural power after state powers had abandoned them.

During the presidency of Franklin Delano Roosevelt (1933-1945), his administration constructed a series of programs called the "New Deal," which permanently altered the structure of the federal government and reshaped the nation's political and social life. The programs of the New Deal covered nearly every aspect of America's political, social, and economic life, and many proved successful in helping the nation on the road to recovery. For most African Americans the Great Depression had reduced the American Dream to a veritable nightmare. While the New Deal programs provided some advancements, they reinforced local patterns of racism, they tolerated the widespread practice of paying African Americans lower wages than whites for working the same jobs, and they allowed discrimination in their hiring practices. African Americans would later sing the praises of the New Deal because it established the presidency as the most important center of authority in the federal government and diminished the sovereignty of local and state governments. This shift of governmental power would greatly facilitate the Civil Rights Movement decades later.

When World War II broke out, African Americans again determined to use conflict to improve their lot, but this time by making demands on the federal government. When a group of African Americans threatened to march on Washington, D.C. in 1941, the Fair Employment Practice Commission was established resulting in an important step towards a government commitment to racial equality in the workforce. As in World War I the manufacturing needs of the nation in World War II created jobs that drew African Americans from the South in large numbers. This migration again provoked race riots when black workers began moving into all white neighborhoods in the North. The Detroit race riot of 1943 left 34 persons dead, 25 of whom were African Americans. In efforts to thwart racial tensions, the Congress of Racial Equality was established in 1943, thus mobilizing mass resistance to discrimination in a manner which had never before occurred. World War II itself aroused a defiant spirit among African Americans and this too would facilitate the Civil Rights Movement.

More than 700,000 African Americans served in the military forces during World War II to find discrimination on every front; however, public and political pressures as well as the recognition that segregated practices wasted manpower began to force military leaders to make practical adjustments. Despite intense racism in the armed services, African Americans began to be awarded higher military ranks and by 1948 the armed services were beginning to be desegregated. This was a major

155

breakthrough which encouraged African Americans to seek military careers. By the 1990s African Americans began to be awarded the highest ranks in the armed services.

In 1954 the United States Supreme Court Decision of Brown v. Board of Education of Topeka struck down the doctrine of "separate but equal" embodied in the 1896 Plessy v. Ferguson Decision. This followed a massive attempt to end segregation that began in 1948 primarily in the South. The Brown Decision, the most important decision ever made by the Supreme Court, reflected the legal efforts of the National Association for the Advancement of Colored People who filed a suit against the school board of Topeka, Kansas. This lawsuit involved a Topeka black girl who had to travel several miles to a black public school even though she lived nearby a white public school. The Supreme Court's unanimous Decision concluded that the "separate but equal" doctrine has no place in the field of public education, and that separate educational facilities are inherently unequal. Although it offered no prescription or guidance as to how desegregation should be accomplished, the Court assumed that it would take place gradually but "with all deliberate speed." Southern politicians established massive resistance to the court order which resulted in 100 southern Congressmen signing a 1956 "manifesto" denouncing the Brown Decision. Moreover, they urged their constituents to defy the Brown Decision thereby establishing a confrontation with federal authority and opening old wounds of state sovereignty. Thus began the war against racial discrimination and the beginning of the Civil Rights Movement, sometimes noted as the "Second Reconstruction" in American history.

Many factors fueled the Civil Rights Movement including several important developments in the philosophical "Cold War" that the United States was waging against the United Soviet Socialist Republics. The federal government was sensitive to American social blights that might serve communist propaganda purposes abroad, and was forced to move into a position of support for civil rights. The black population had grown in the urban areas to synthesize ideas and organizations which could produce effective change. Most importantly, many African Americans with the counsel of several reform groups had come to the realization that civil liberties would not be handed to them for some past loyalties, duties, or meritorious service. Some were ready to risk their lives in order to become agents for change and social justice, and to that end they recognized that a series of confrontations were inevitable. This mind-set and the confrontations which accompanied it are generally identified as the Black Revolution.

The Black Revolution is sometimes traced to a celebrated case in Montgomery, Alabama when on December 1, 1955, a black seamstress named Rosa Parks refused to give up her seat on a Montgomery bus to a white passenger. She thus broke a Jim Crow law that was comparable to those throughout the South. Although she had broken this law before and had been arrested, her arrest this time sparked a bus boycott that lasted more than a year. The success of the boycott was not as important as the fact that a new form of racial protest had been established. African Americans had banned together in the boycott in spite of sustained economic pressures from white Montgomery employers and businessmen. It also elevated Martin Luther King, Jr. to prominence as a new figure and leader in the Civil Rights Movement.

The Montgomery bus boycott was the first example of a black community mobilizing *en masse* to confront racial segregation. Its non-violent approach would be emulated throughout the Civil Rights Movement and spearheaded by Martin Luther King, Jr. Early in 1960 "sit-in" demonstrations began which forced merchants to integrate their facilities, and it gained great support from northern whites especially on college campuses. This resulted in hundreds of African Americans, including women and children, being arrested or detained without regard to space limitations in southern jailhouses. The "freedom rides" began the following year where both whites and African Americans traveled by bus throughout the South in efforts to force desegregation of bus stations. The "sit-in" demonstrations and the "freedom rides" were often met with violence from local whites. Federal marshals had to be called in most cases because the local officials would often side with the white mobs. These confrontations were widely viewed on national television to horrify many whites who had somehow been oblivious to the inhumanity of racial injustice. White Americans also saw the manifestations of racial injustice with white police using attack dogs, tear gas, electric cattle prods, and fire hoses against peaceful black demonstrators including small children.

In the meantime the federal courts were confronted by a series of incidents involving the desegregation of public schools, colleges, and universities. The first incident to receive national attention was in 1957 in Little Rock, Arkansas where for the first time in history the President of the United States sent federal troops to restore order and to ensure that a court order to admit black students was obeyed. Similar incidents occurred in Mississippi in 1962 and Alabama in 1963. Southern white mobs directed sporadic violence against black students and their supporters, and many whites were determined that southern schools would remain segregated even at the cost of education for white students.

By the mid-1960s it was evident that radical changes were taking place; however, it was too late to defuse resentment from generations of racism and economic repression which had been smoldering since the 1896 Plessy v. Ferguson Decision. Race riots broke out in the black section of Los Angeles in 1965 and subsequently spread to nearly every major city in the United States. In the summer of 1966 alone there were 43 race riots, the most notable of which were in Cleveland and Chicago. Eight race riots occurred in the nation during the following summer when Detroit headed the bloody list. As in most race riots, more African Americans than whites lost their lives while the National Guard had to be called in to quell the disturbances. The riots were characterized by looting, attacking whites in their automobiles, sniping against the police, and a massive burning and destruction of property in the black neighborhoods.

The 1960s were also characterized by a series of assassinations of public figures including President John F. Kennedy in 1963, Muslim leader Malcolm X in 1965, Attorney General Robert F. Kennedy and Martin Luther King, Jr. in 1968, and several local civil rights leaders. When Martin Luther King, Jr. was assassinated in Memphis, Tennessee, the entire nation mourned in a state of shock. King was greatly admired worldwide and was an outstanding leader in the Civil Rights Movement. In the days following his death, major riots broke out in more than 60 American cities. The aftermath of the riot in a black section of Washington, D.C. was described by one observer as resembling a burnt-out war zone.

Although the prevailing response to the turmoil of the 1960s was an American conservative reaction, revolutionary change continued to improve the social and economic conditions of many African Americans. For example, African American women began to take more assertive roles of leadership; African Americans began to exercise political power in the right to vote; a war on poverty was launched which generated food stamps, rent supplements to the poor, and Medicare and Medicaid; and the United States Department of Labor issued Affirmative Action rules. More African Americans began secure employment on levels commensurate with whites, public accommodations began to be extended without regard to race, and public schools throughout the nation embarked on the painful road of desegregation.

For the next two decades African Americans were engaged in consolidating the gains of the Civil Rights Movement while at the same time they experienced a period of disillusionment. The struggle then moved to the courts where litigation was slow and sometimes painful. African Americans found that it was one effort to establish a law against unequal treatment, but it was quite another to implement it. The black struggle captured the attention of other groups in America who had received unequal treatment: Native Americans, Latin Americans, homosexuals, the elderly, and women. The black struggle for equality therefore encouraged all Americans to demand civil liberties and equal treatment in all facets of the society.

Black America was greatly impacted when Ronald Reagan became President of the United States in 1981 as his administration has been noted as the most conservative of the twentieth-century. The recession of 1982 reemphasized that despite the gains of the Civil Rights Movement, African Americans were still the "last to be hired and the first to be fired." Structural changes in the workplace were also shaping an "Information Age" economy where downsizing and layoffs became a common occurrence. Many African American workers long accustomed to job security in manufacturing suddenly lost their jobs to overseas markets. The Reagan era also encouraged the reversal of affirmative action gains which gave some parity in employment practices, it was responsible for the reversal of federal set-a-side funds for educational and social programs which were designed to address decades of black deprivation, and most importantly, it promoted a Supreme Court which began to issue conservative interpretations of the 1965 voting rights laws. The Reagan administration promulgated a "race neutral society" in the wake of efforts still brewing to establish racial parity in American society; it therefore largely contributed to the period of disillusionment following the Civil Rights Movement.

The period of disillusionment is reflected in a May 1996 survey conducted for *The New Yorker* magazine. The survey shows that 59 percent of a cross section of African American adults feel that the American Dream is impossible to achieve in a nation that continues to deny equal opportunity. Most African Americans in the 1990s are convinced that the plight of black America is worsening and half believe that race relations will never be better. While the African American middle-class has made great social and economic strides since the Civil Rights Movement, a third of all African Americans continue to live in dire poverty. These conditions are supported in J. L. Hochschild's book, *Facing Up to the American Dream (1995)*. Hochschild's study shows that despite their gains middle-class African Americans have become disillusioned and embittered about the American Dream while poor African Americans believe in it as much as poor African Americans did 30 years ago. However, *The New Yorker* survey found that "48 percent of African Americans believe that the failure of blacks to take advantage of the opportunities available to them constitutes a greater problem than discrimination by whites" (Anderson, 1996).

Some observers contend that there are dangerous parallels between the periods of southern redemption (1877-1896) and the Reagan era (1981-1993). Each period followed a revolution where African Americans achieved unprecedented social, political, and economic gain; each period reflected a backlash of white conservative reaction; and each period abused the power of the ballot to either whip blacks back into submission or to maintain the political status quo. Herein lies the value and the importance of studying history as well as the classic realization that "those who do not study history are doomed to repeat it." The fallout of southern redemption ushered in more than half a century of turmoil and social upheaval as the nation approached the year 1900. America's challenge is to thwart any such reversals as we approach the year 2000.

It can be argued that the American Dream as postulated by the founding fathers of the United States was realized in just a few decades after they established the Constitution. However, the founding fathers had a narrow focus for the propertied few which was reflected in their aspirations. The beauty of the American Dream is that it is dynamic and not static. It therefore encourages each generation of Americans to aspire to new levels of perfection which prompt them to be the best that they can be within that domain. African Americans remain the last group to approach assimilation in the United States, yet they have brought forth a rich history of lessons for mutual progress. Without full recognition of those lessons, there can be little progress.

# References

Anderson, J. (1996) Black and Blue in *The New Yorker* April 29 - May 6, 1996, pp. 62 - 64.

Bacote, C. A. Negro Proscriptions, Protests, and Proposed Solutions in Georgia, 1880-1908. In *The Negro In the South Since 1865*, C. E. Wynes ed. (1965) University, Alabama: University of Alabama Press.

Bennett, L. Jr. (1962) *Before The Mayflower*, Chicago: Johnson Publishing Co., Inc.

*Biological Sketches from Black & Proud part 4*, (1970) Cleveland, Ohio: Public Affairs, General Electric Lamp Division.

Blassingame, J. W. (1972) *The Slave Community*, New York: Oxford University Press.

Brown, W. W. (1867) *The Negro in the American Rebellion*, Boston: Lee & Shepard.

Burchard, P. (1965) *One Gallant Rush*, New York: St. Martin's Press.

Chapman, A. (1968) *Black Voices*, New York: The New American Library.

Clark, T. D. and A. D. Kirwan (1967) *The South Since Appomattox*, New York: Oxford University Press.

Cleveland Gazette. January 31, 1885.

Chase P. & Collier W.M. (1970) *Justice Denied*, New York: Harcourt, Brace, & World, Inc.

Cornish, D. (1970) Second-Class Soldiers. In W.M. Chace & P. Collier (Eds.), *Justice Denied* (pp. 141-151). New York: Harcourt, Brace & World, Inc.

Douglass, F. (1855) *My Bondage and My Freedom*, New York: Miller, Orton, & Mulligan.

DuBois, W.E.B. (1903) *Souls of Black Folk*, Chicago: A.C. McClurg and Co.

Fogel, R. W. and S. L. Engerman (1974) *Time on the Cross*, Boston-Toronto: Little, Brown and Co.

Franklin, J. H. (1961) *Reconstruction: After the Civil War*, Chicago and London: The University of Chicago Press.

Franklin, J. H. (1974) *From Slavery to Freedom: A History of Negro Americans*, New York: Alfred A. Knopf.

Franklin, J. H. Jim Crow Goes To School: The Genesis of Legal Segregation in the South. In *The Negro In The South Since 1865*, C. E. Wynes ed. (1965) University, Alabama: University of Alabama Press.

Frazier, E. F. (1932) *The Free Negro Family*, Nashville, Tenn.: Fisk University Press.

Frazier, E. F. (1963) *The Negro Church in America*, New York: Schoken Books.

Higginson, T.W. (1962) *Army Life in a Black Regiment*, Boston: Beacon Press.

Hill, S. S. Jr. (1980) *The South and the North in American Religion*, Athens, GA.

Hochschild, J. L. (1995) *Facing Up to the American Dream: Race, Class, and the Soul of the Nation*, Princeton, NJ: Princeton University Press.

Irvine, R. (1966) *The Higher and Professional Education of African Americans: 1774-1865.* Unpublished manuscript.

*Journal of Negro History Vol. LV, No. 3*, (1970) Washington, D.C. The Association For the Study of Negro Life and History, Inc.

Katz, W. L. (1987) *The Black West*, Seattle: Open Hand Publishing, Inc.

Lapp, R. M. (1977) *Blacks in Gold Rush California*, New Haven and Lond: Yale University Press.

Leckie, W. H. (1967) *The Buffalo Soldiers*, Norman: The University of Oklahoma Press.

Lewis, E. M. The Political Mind of the Negro. In *The Negro In The South Since 1865*, C. E. Wynes ed. (1965) University, Alabama: University of Alabama Press.

Lincoln, C. E. (1967) *The Negro Pilgrimage in America*, New York: Bantan Pathfinder Editions.

Logan, R. (1965) *The Betrayal of the Negro from Rutherford B. Hayes to Woodrow Wilson*, New York: Collier Books.

McCague, J. (1968) *The Second Rebellion: The Story of the New York City Draft Riots of 1863*, New York: The Dial Press, Inc.

McPherson, J. M. (1965) *The Negro's Civil War*, New York: Pantheon Books.

Miller, K. (1908) *Race Adjustment*, New York: The Neale Publishing Co.

Meltzer, M. (1967) *Thaddeus Stevens and the Fight for Negro Rights*, New York: Thomas Y. Crowell Co.

New York Times, September 29, 1862.

New York Times, January 6, 1863.

Osofsky, G. (1967) *The Burden of Race*, New York: Harper and Row.

*Philadelphia Times* (N.D.) Quoted in *The Arkansas Weekly Mansion* (p.326). November 10, ,1883 Nation XXXII.

Pearson, E.W. ed. (1969) *Letters from Port Royal 1862-1868*, New York: Arno Press and The New York Times.

Pease, W. H. and J. H. (1971) The Negro Convention Movement. In N. I. Huggins, M. Kilson, & D. M. Fox (eds.), *Key Issues in the Afro-American Experience* (pp. 191-205). New York: Harcourt Brace Javanovich, Inc.

Quarles, B. (1953) *The Negro in the Civil War*, New York: Russell & Russell.

Quarles, B. (1964) *The Negro in the Making of America*, New York: The Macmillan Co.

Quarles, B. (1968) *Frederick Douglass, Great Lives Observed* Englewood Cliffs, N.J.: Prentice-Hall Inc.

Raboteau, A.J. (1978) *Slave Religion*, New York: Oxford Press.

Roen, S.R. (1960) Personality and Negro Intelligence. In *Journal of Abnormal and Social Psychology*.

Rose, W.L. (1964) *Rehearsal for Reconstruction*, Indianapolis: Bobbs-Merrill Company.

Savage, W. S. (1976) *Blacks in the West*, Westpoint, CT:. Greenwood Press.

Stampp, K.M. (1965) *The Era of Reconstruction 1865-1877* New York: Vantage Books.

Turner, H. M. (1913) *The Negro in Slavery, War, and Peace*, Philadelphia: A.M.E. Book Concern, a reprint from the A.M.E. Review.

Tyler, A. F. (1944) *Freedoms Ferment*, New York: The University of Minnesota Press.

Van Evrie, J. H., M.D. (1868) *White Supremacy and Negro Subordination*, New York: Van Evrie, Horton & Co.

Wade, R. C. ed. (1965) Slavery in the Cities. In *The Negro In American Life*, Boston: Houghton Mifflin Co.

Wesley, C. H. and P. W. Romero. (1967) *International Library of Negro Life and History; Negro Americans in the Civil War*, New York: Publisher's Co., Inc.

Wiley, B. I. (1965) *Southern Negroes 1861-1865*, New Haven: Yale University Press.

Williams, G. W. (1883) *The History of The Negro Race in America Vol. II*, New York: G.P. Putnam's Sons.

Wish, H. (1938) Slave Disloyalty Under the Confederacy. In *The Journal of Negro History*, Vol. 23.

Woodard, C. Vann (1966) *Reunion and Reaction: The Compromise of 1877 and the End of Reconstruction*, Boston: Little, Brown.

Woodard, C. Vann (1966) *The Strange Career of Jim Crow*, New York: Oxford University Press.

Woodward, W. E. (1928) *Meet General Grant*, New York: H. Liveright.

# Index

90
Brownsville, Texas 151
Bruce, Blanche K. 100, 108, 121
Buchanan, James 57
Buffalo Soldiers 49-53
Burgess, John William 148
Butler, Benjamin 75
C
Calhoun, John C. 44, 148
California 7, 10, 44, 46
Camp Meigs, Massachusetts 72
Canada 71
Caribbean Islands 9
Carney, William Harvey 73
Carson, Kit 48, 53
Charleston, South Carolina xvi, 2, 39, 65, 66, 72, 73
Cherokee Bill 48, 50
Cherokee Nation xix, 50
Cheyenne War 48, 52
Chicago, Illinois 2, 7, 41, 113, 131, 152, 158
Chisom Trail 46
Christianity 36, 37, 39, 41, 77
Cincinnati, Ohio 2, 11, 81, 112, 113
Civil Disobedience 14
Civil Rights Act of 1875 122
Civil Rights Movement 155-160
Civil War xx, xxii, 1, 5, 11, 13, 37-39, 46, 61, 63, 68, 70, 73, 75-78, 80, 82, 90, 91, 93, 95, 96, 100, 101, 103, 106-108, 110, 113, 115, 120, 125, 126, 131, 144, 148, 149

Clark University 111
Clark, Peter Humphries 101, 111
Cleveland, Ohio 115, 158
Coffin, Levi 26
Cold War 156
Colorado 46, 48, 52
Colored Methodist Episcopal Church 131
Comanches 113
Compromise of 1877 121, 125
Confederacy 73, 75, 80, 84-86, 89, 90
Confederate Troops 65, 73, 81, 82, 86, 87, 91
Confiscation Act of 1862 71
Congress of Racial Equality 155
Congressional Medal of Honor 52, 53, 65, 73
Connecticut 91
Conyers, James 115
Cook, James F. 40
Cooper Union 83
Creek Indians 50
Crockett, David 48
Crogman, William H. 111
Crow Indians 48
Custer, George A. 53
Cuyahoga County 115
D
Daddy Grace 154
Dakotas 48, 52
Dartmouth College 9
Davis, Jefferson 73, 75, 87, 108, 148
Declaration of Independence 93, 101